Banff National Park Hiking Guide

The Best Twelve Trails for a Serene Escape in Canada

Vera Fuller

TABLE OF CONTENTS

INTRODUCTION

Hiking didn't just save my marriage and family life; it saved my life too! I know this might sound harsh or too honest, maybe even a shocking statement to some, but I'm telling you the truth!

Before I start telling you about the chain of events that led me to this moment in my life, I will paint a picture of my life a few years ago: Now let us imagine there is a woman whose life was consumed by a high-stress finance job. This was me, a mother of four girls, a husband, and a job that left little time for anything else.

Every day, I had meetings, deadlines, and a to-do list that would go on and on. It left me feeling overwhelmed and exhausted almost every day. Can you even imagine how unhappy I was? In a few months, I found myself detached from the world around me.

I didn't pay attention to my husband or my kids, and I was unable to enjoy the pleasures of life. I took all of it for granted, and that is how I found myself absolutely miserable all the time.

Days turned into weeks, and weeks turned into months, and as much as I wouldn't like to point this out, the months turned even into years. My stress began to take a toll on me. It was a dark moment when my mental and physical health suffered. I was facing anxiety, constant insomnia, and constant mood swings, and I was still functioning.

I tried to work it out! I collaborated with a therapist, I went out, and I tried to find a way out of it—a way to find myself inside the city and with other people. Nothing ever helped, and I felt stuck.

I could not break free from the stress, and the exhaustion had consumed me. I know you might feel the same right now. I understand your pain. You might be successful in your career and have a comfortable lifestyle, but you still feel like something needs to be added.

I know you think you're not living life to its fullest potential, and this can lead you to restlessness and dissatisfaction. You have an underlying desire for meaning and purpose that craves adventure and new things.

There might be some of you that are facing burnout from your work. Or you might feel bored in your current routine, a monotony where you want to explore new places, or you might have minimal access to green spaces and nature, which is the worst-case scenario. I know because I was there too. I know the pain you feel, and I have felt it too.

Until one moment, it was a routine checkup at my doctor, which I barely made, and my work demanded it from me because I was running low on energy and was failing to meet my deadlines. And I'm so thankful for the moment: The catalyst that triggered me into a new life.

My doctor thought that I needed more rest or that my health anxiety and constant stress levels might be the surge of me. It might drive me to my demise. And I know that this might not sound too harsh, but it was the switch that I needed.

I know you also had a moment like this, which is why you are here now. This catalyst moment is why you're reading this introduction. I know that it's never the title that sells a book. On the contrary, it's always the moment you have felt too. The moment when you know everything has changed for you. And I welcome you to the new life you are going to experience.

You have reached the point where you learn about a way to reconnect with nature and find solace in nature. This book is here to guide you.

I have written this book with all levels of hikers in mind, with detailed instructions for trails, trail information tips, and safe and efficient hiking ideas. I also have insights into the emotional, mental, and physical benefits of nature. But more on that later.

In fact, it was a turning point in my life once I did that routine checkup at my doctor's office. I took a two-week vacation, packed up all of my four girls and my husband, and took them on a national park camping holiday. Finally, after almost two years, I felt serene and at ease. I know you want to feel like this too!

I felt that I had escaped the stress of daily life, found adventure, and finally achieved a sense of balance and a sense of well-being due to my connection with nature. And I know that you can find this too. In fact, this guidebook doesn't give you just hiking information. It will provide you with a more profound sense of belonging to nature, show you the benefits of spending time inside of nature, and offer you insight into how to hike and reduce stress. You will improve your mental health, and all of this will give you a sense of purpose.

As you might expect, the knowledge and years it has taken me to accumulate; I have been hiking since I was a child, but in the last ten years, I have taken to national parks. Hiking there with my family and enjoying life; that is how long it took me to gather all the knowledge I have here for you.

I also have some friends I have pushed into the hiking community or whom I have shown camping as a way of coping with their stress levels at work and life, which have completely changed their lifestyles. Imagine that one of them has moved their whole family of five into a camper van and only works from home during the winter and lives a van life from Spring to Autumn.

You might not want the same for your family, but the goal is the end result you get from finally achieving the catalyst moment and moving on to become a better version of yourself. In fact, the end result of reading this book is gaining new and practical hiking skills.

You will finally have some self-confidence, not just in your looks but in your abilities, and you will feel empowered to face new challenges in your life. Finally, you will also see the many physical and mental benefits of spending time in nature, not just physical fitness, which is the most apparent one, but also reduced stress levels, lower anxiety, and a sense of well-being.

As a hiker of ten years, a mother of four, a wife, and someone who has pushed numerous people into a new life and made them try out camping and hiking as a way of life, I think I would be the best one to teach you.

You might think that achieving your end goal will be easy. On the contrary, it took me ten years to finally reach the ultimate work-life balance I have yearned for. This is also why you need some time to reach your goal too.

In fact, it was much more challenging to achieve our goals back in the day. Gathering information, knowing where to hike, how to hike, and general information about national parks was much harder to come by. The internet only recently became so open to sharing hiking and trail information, which is why my long experience in hiking and numerous years spent researching will reveal to you everything you need to know. Even what modern hikers might not know!

I have written this book to help you reach your goals, not just hiking-wise but also as a parent and as another human being. I wish you all the best. I have prepared this list of the 12 best hikes in Banff National Park, which will help you not just to prepare for these hikes but also give you all the information you need.

Still, the goal is to prepare you physically and mentally for what is to come on these hikes and give you a push into the hiking life. That is by giving you all the tips in the formation you need. Therefore, be prepared for this journey, but don't be scared because it is ultimately what we are made for.

EMBARKING ON A JOURNEY

We crave a life of adventure; we want to live without regrets and make the most of our lives. It is human nature. We want to finally disconnect from our busy lives and find peace, solace, and nature. We wish to experience new places, landscapes, and cultures.

That is exactly why we are here, wanting to explore Banff National Park and wanting to embark on a journey that will take us to the new us. That is exactly why I am writing this book. I want to showcase the extraordinary destination that this National Park is. I wish to show the awe-inspiring fusion of majestic mountains, endless skies, and picturesque lakes, all that with an alpine forest, which leaves one breathless.

That is why in this chapter, I will delve deep into the wonders of this National Park, but that is not all. We will witness and marvel at the solace peaks, pristine lakes, verdant forests, and abundant wildlife this region has to offer. Finally, we will uncover the hidden treasures of hiking and immersing ourselves in the vastness of nature.

But what is it that makes nature so medicinal to us? This chapter right here will also tell you why hiking is so helpful to the human spirit. You will experience numerous therapeutic effects of it, but you will also discover yourself and how positively it can impact our physical, mental, and emotional well-being. That is why I ask you to come along and embark on this journey that will inspire us and rejuvenate our souls.

Disconnection From Nature

Now imagine yourself ten years from now. Do you see a happy, healthy person or a stressed individual who just wants to make ends meet? As a hiker, I see myself doing exactly that - hiking with my friends, family, and partner and enjoying my life. For you, I wish you the same. I want to share a love for nature, not just hiking, with everyone.

I want to teach everyone that we all need to live with nature's cycles and enjoy nature's company. And in the next section, I will also show you how and why nature significantly impacts our daily lives and why being so out of touch and disconnected from nature, as if we were not part of her, is terrible for us.

Not being in sync with our natural cycles and not enjoying nature is also one of the ailments of today's society. In fact, loving Mother Earth is what grounds us to be human.

We're running to pick up our kids from practice, running to reach deadlines not to be late for work. Running to reach home before rush hour and finally, running from ourselves.

We're constantly running, and we are increasingly running away from nature. We are becoming disconnected from her every day, more and more. We don't listen to the cycles of nature. We are not in touch with her, and we are constantly out of sync with our own lives.

We barely see greenery, and all of this is why a changing environment that offers stress will definitely impact our mood, nervous and immune systems. That is why we are constantly feeling anxious, sad, helpless, and even sick.

A more soothing environment that lives in the cycle with nature at a slower pace is what we need. It reverses the damage our bodies have been pushed under. It doesn't matter what culture, age, gender, or anything else for that matter, you are from. All humans find nature to be pleasing and calming!

In fact, is there a better place to retreat when you're feeling stressed, sad, or out of place than nature itself? I think not, and I think you agree with me too. We all know that modern life has become disconnected from nature. It's not even a question anymore!

On the contrary, we now need to mitigate the problems that this type of lifestyle and fast lifestyle have caused. This disconnection will definitely impact the well-being of every human not living in sync with nature. Will you be one of them? We need to remember the importance of going back to nature!

It offers us better overall health but not just that. It offers insight into who we are, offers us a place to ease our mental health problems, work on our physical health, and better our immune system. I thank nature for that!

Finally, to end this section, I must remind you that nature is the first step in embarking on this journey. That goes not just for Banff National Park but for any other national park out there. Living with nature is a goal we need to reach, even if it might be just one day every month. We know that life with nature will ease us and help us!

The Benefits of Hiking and the Great Outdoors

Who doesn't know about the numerous benefits of going outside? Even a short walk in the park can make you feel better almost any day.

As I have previously discussed, the benefits of hiking or just spending time in nature are numerous. In fact, spending time in nature doesn't just mean hiking. No, it means camping, fishing, hunting, walking, backpacking, kayaking, swimming, birding, and so on. Be aware that not just hiking has numerous perks but also other forms of engagement with nature.

In fact, hiking and spending time in the great outdoors can and will provide numerous benefits to you. These include physical, mental, and emotional well-being, as well as a sense of peace. Here are some of the critical benefits of hiking and being in nature:

- **Better health:** One can use hiking as a great way to exercise. It is a full-body workout that strengthens muscles and improves cardiovascular health.
- **Reduces stress:** We all know that spending time in nature lowers stress and anxiety. That is because being surrounded by greenery and fresh air helps you calm down, reduces cortisol, and improves your mood.

- **Boost mental health:** Being outside improves cognitive function and creativity, and it can improve memory, increase attention span, and enhance your problem-solving skills.
- **Raise the immune system:** Spending time outside in the natural world helps boost your immune system because you breathe in phytoncides, which help you gain strength.
- **Connection:** Spending time outside will help you cultivate a deeper connection with the natural world by giving you a sense of awe, gratitude, and environmentalism.

I love everything about hiking, and I am sure you will love it too! From the comforting warmth of sunshine on your face to the sound of wind rushing through the trees and the soft earthy feel of the trail beneath your boots. Can you even imagine these sensory experiences not only bring joy? It's not just happiness, they also have numerous health benefits.

This plethora of health benefits extends beyond the physical exercise. Being in nature can provide emotional and mental relief, which we all need. It will help reduce stress levels and promote a sense of well-being.

Overall, it doesn't matter whether it's a short walk in a local park or a multi-day trek in a wilderness area. The benefits of being in nature are well worth the effort. Therefore, if you are waiting for a push into hiking or a sign that you can finally start to hike and put yourself out there, this is your sign.

In fact, read through this book and this guide to learn the basics about hiking and start hiking in your backyard. You don't have to hike inside national parks; you can do it in smaller parks and even near your home. But more on the hiking basics in the next section. Let this talk about the benefits of hiking be your sign to start engaging yourself toward becoming a hiker yourself.

The Beauty of Banff National Park

Before we start talking about the unparalleled beauty this amazing place offers, we first need to focus on some basics about the park. Therefore, we will first explore the most important information: Banff National Park is a large natural area in Canada with beautiful scenery and wildlife.

It became a National Park in 1887 and covered over 2,500 square miles in the Rocky Mountains in Alberta. There are other parks nearby in British Columbia and Alberta, and much of the surrounding area is also protected. That is how magnificent the region is, and Banff is at its entrance.

The park's nearest town and headquarters is Banff town, about 80 miles from Calgary. This section of the Canadian Rocky Mountains is famous for its stunning landscapes, diverse plants and animals, and ongoing geologic processes.

As you might have seen, Banff is truly stunning. What you haven't experienced so far, and I hope you will soon manage to see, is that Banff National Park is an incredibly beautiful place. It is where majestic mountains, clear lakes, and lush forests come together in a breathtaking landscape.

I wish to show you the beauty of this National Park! And my goal is to paint a vivid picture of what Banff has to offer, how beautiful it is, and how stunning the views here can be. I want to introduce it, so you have a basis for understanding this National Park and for further reading through this book. I believe you need to understand how beautiful this place is and, most importantly, why it needs to be protected.

Hiking here is one thing, but enjoying the beauty of this unique National Park is another. That is exactly why we must protect these rugged mountains, lakes, and forests. Our goal should be to save them for the next generation to come.

Surely the thing you will enjoy most during your visit to Banff National Park is the landscapes, and if you still haven't decided whether or not to visit it, let this description of mine be the push you need. Only this way, while visiting it, will you be able to enjoy the captivating beauty it offers fully.

The terrain in Banff National Park is mainly rugged and mountainous, with a significant portion of it being part of the Rockies' Main Ranges section. The mountains are composed of sedimentary rocks and have a toothlike appearance due to glaciation, particularly in the western section along the Continental Divide.

Banff National Park offers a beautiful view of the Rocky Mountains, with peaks rising above 10,000 feet, including Mount Columbia and Mount Sir Douglas. The park has active glaciers, including a portion of the extensive Columbia Icefield. It is home to several dozen mammal species, such as bears, elk, moose, deer, wolves, coyotes, pumas, bighorn sheep, and mountain goats. Banff National Park is a place where you can breathe in crisp and fresh air and marvel at the sights and sounds of nature.

Apart from the stunning views and breathtaking landscapes, Banff National Park boasts a rich array of wildlife. People have lived in this region for almost 11,000 years. In 1883, employees of the Canadian Pacific Railway discovered the cluster of natural hot springs, leading to the park's creation as Canada's first National Park under the Rocky Mountains Park Act.

The park's size was extended and given its present name in 1930, and it has since become Canada's most famous National Park. Today, it is an internationally renowned alpine sports location. Whether you're an experienced hiker or a beginner, Banff National Park offers a world of adventure and discovery, with hundreds of miles of hiking trails, winter sports venues at Banff and Lake Louise, and a variety of other recreational activities available for visitors.

In fact, numerous people out there consider Banff one of the most beautiful places on Earth. But what makes it so beautiful? Is it the majestic mountains, the glaciers, or the clear lakes? Well, it's most probably a combination of all of these factors.

Banff National Park has, as said before, majestic mountains that rise above rugged terrain and numerous towering peaks. It also has to offer glaciers and ice fields. In fact, it is one of the rare regions that still offer glaciers. One can enjoy lakes that feed from the ice, with the iconic turquoise Lake Louise and Moraine Lake. You can also see diverse wildlife and enjoy scenic hikes here.

Now that we have seen the numerous benefits nature and spending time with her can give us, featuring less anxiety and stress to better immune systems, we can definitely conclude that a visit to Banff National Park or any national park would be a great way to spend our time! The goal isn't just to enjoy ourselves. Oh no, the goal would be to work on our health and relationships with the people we bring with us.

Conclusion

I hope I have introduced Banff National Park in the best light, as it should be shown. This place is truly a section where mountains rule and lakes stun with their beauty. I also hope you have seen the beauty of hiking and spending time in nature.

That doesn't just go hiking with our families. It goes for solo hiking and hiking with friends, pets, and significant others. Still, hiking isn't just going outside. No, hiking requires specific preparations, and that is why the next chapter will cover the essentials and safety considerations while hiking. Therefore, stay tuned to learn how to hike, regardless of your group, with a key focus on Banff National Park.

PREPARATION IS KEY

Hiking isn't just about reaching peaks and taking pictures. On the contrary, hiking is a pastime where you enjoy nature and yourself.

It is a way to connect with yourself, find out who you truly are, and spend time with your loved ones, regardless of who you plan on hiking with. Also, whatever route you choose, the goal is to enjoy yourself and not push yourself too hard.

In this chapter, we will cover the basics of hiking and how preparation is vital. That goes not just for intermediate and knowledgeable hikers but the key for beginners too. In fact, beginners need to prepare more than anyone else.

Here, I will consider the safety side of hiking, how to select your trail, plan your trip, and what gear you need for hiking in Banff National Park. As I said above, hiking isn't just any physical activity or a sport. To most people, it has changed their lives as it has changed mine.

I believe it's a truly transformative experience that will definitely help you find a more positive outlook on your life. It also comes with certain risks! In fact, we will explore the importance of safety, considering the numerous safety hazards while hiking. These tips and plans will make a difference for you!

They will be the difference between a great hiking experience and a dangerous one, both for you and your group. Another friendly reminder is that you do need to have a certain knowledge of the trail before you venture on it. And that doesn't just include safety considerations but also the duration, length, and other information you might need for your group.

Therefore, if you wish to stay safe, choose the perfect path for you, and plan your visit successfully. Make sure to read through this chapter and consider what it is that you might be missing in your hiking plan. In the end, make sure you have considered all of these points before setting out on your journey. Also, ensure you have all the safety knowledge, planning, and gear you need to hike in Banff National Park.

Safety Considerations for Every Hike

Too many hikers nowadays find themselves in uncalled-for situations, which is why my book needs to cover some basic safety tips for hiking. They might seem like common sense to the intermediate and knowledgeable hikers. Still, I see too many newbie hikers that find themselves in bad situations due to a lack of knowledge. And I want to prevent it!

Remember that all uncalled-for and bad situations that might happen on the trail start out with minor mishaps. It might be that rain soaks the trail, or your water bottle starts leaking, and then you become cold and wet.

Due to this, you soon start to shiver and head back but can't find your trail. Or it could be that you slip on wet grass, and in a few moments, you will find yourself in for a really long night on the trail. Instead, you could have been safe and sound, eating your meal after your hike.

Next, we will cover a few considerations before every hike:

- **Overnight preparation:** Unexpected situations may occur on any hike, and problems such as getting lost or having an injury can delay your hike. That is why you should always have all the necessary gear and supplies to spend an overnight in the wild.

- **Let someone know:** Another key role in hiking is letting someone know where you are going if something unexpected happens. This person will know your plans and can alert the authorities, who can then organize a search and rescue operation.

- **Research your route in advance:** This helps you understand the terrain, the expected weather conditions, and potential hazards or obstacles. This knowledge can help you prepare for the hike by bringing the right gear and supplies and can also help you avoid dangerous situations by choosing a route that matches your skill level and experience. Be aware of any trail closures or restrictions as well as any rules and regulations of the area you'll be hiking in.

- **Bring snacks and extra water:** You want to keep yourself hydrated and fed during the hike. Dehydration and fatigue can lead to poor decision-making! Bring enough water to last for the entire hike, as well as snacks.

- **Not interacting with wildlife:** This is important to maintain your own safety as well as the safety of the animals. Wild animals can be unpredictable and potentially dangerous if provoked. Please do not attempt to feed or approach them.

- **Starting your day early:** This tip can help you avoid the heat of the day. Starting early also gives you plenty of daylight hours to complete your hike and deal with any unexpected situations that may arise. Additionally, starting early can help you avoid crowds on popular hiking trails.

- **Carry a whistle:** This is important because it can be used to signal for help in case of an emergency. A whistle's sound carries much farther than a person's voice, making it an effective way to communicate when in distress.

- **Do not wear headphones:** It is crucial to stay aware of your surroundings while hiking. Headphones can block out important sounds, such as approaching wildlife or other hikers, which can put you in danger.

- **Agree on an emergency plan:** This is important because it ensures that everyone in your hiking group knows what to do in case of an emergency.

- **Prepare yourself physically:** Hiking can be physically demanding, especially if you are attempting a longer or more challenging trail. Ensure that you are in good physical condition before heading out.

Believe me when I tell you, physical conditioning is an important aspect of preparing for any hiking trip. It's essential to be in good shape and have adequate endurance. If there is one goal? It is to tackle the challenges of the trail.

I recommend that you prepare yourself by gradually increasing your activity level. You can do so by building up your endurance. In fact, this is key before attempting more challenging hikes. I do not recommend undertaking strenuous hikes while still a beginner. I know it might sound basic, but this knowledge can help prevent injuries.

If your goal is more strenuous hikes, I recommend starting with moderate hikes at the beginning of the season. Only then should you gradually build up your endurance over time. That will help you develop strength and stamina. In the end, let that not be the only recommendation. It's important to listen to your body! Do not push yourself too hard too soon.

You will also have to prepare for the specific challenges of the trail you'll be hiking. That includes researching the trail. This activity aims to determine its difficulty level and any potential hazards. I recommend a trail that matches your ability level!

Choose Your Trail

It doesn't matter if you are hiking to exercise, trying out a new activity, or spending time with your group or inside nature. The main thing is that you are out on the trail. Still, not all people know which trail is right for them, and that is precisely why I will help you figure out how to pick the best hiking trail for you.

This is a guide with considerations concerning your abilities and knowledge in terms of hiking. As you might know, there are numerous difficulty levels and hiking resources that can both help you become a better hiker and be dangerous for you in the worst-case scenario. I will show you how to choose the suitable hike for you, what considerations to take into account, and which difficulty levels might be appropriate for you.

First and foremost, you should consider your own experience level and physical fitness. That is the base for every hiker! You will need to be honest with yourself about your abilities and choose a trail that matches them. Needless to say, if you are new to hiking or have limited physical endurance, there are still options.

Another key consideration when selecting a trail is often forgotten. It is the season and weather conditions. Certain trails may be more difficult or even unsafe to hike. That goes during certain times of the year, like winter or bad weather, such as heavy rainfall or snowy or icy conditions. That is why checking weather reports can help you determine whether a particular trail is safe and suitable for you!

When selecting a trail, things to consider include the terrain, elevation gain, and overall difficulty level. As you might expect, some trails may have steep inclines, rocky terrain, or narrow paths that can be challenging for some hikers. Not all hikers engage in these trails; others may require specialized gear, such as crampons or ice axes, to navigate safely.

To determine which difficulty level is right for you, consider your experience and fitness level. But not just that, the other factors mentioned above should be considered too. If you are new to hiking or have limited endurance, starting with shorter and less challenging trails is generally best. Only then should you gradually build up your strength and stamina.

That is the beauty of hiking. You have to work for it. As you become more experienced and physically fit, you can then take on longer and more challenging trails. These often offer a greater sense of adventure and accomplishment. Ultimately, the key is choosing a trail you feel comfortable with. What does that trail look like? It allows you to enjoy the beauty and serenity of nature while staying safe and healthy.

Different parks have different guides, websites, and even people rating hiking trails' difficulty differently. Needless to say, there is no unified way of rating hiking trails, or there's no unified system for rating them so far.

Some might use numbers or letters, but most of them are rated as easy, moderate, or strenuous. That is the basic system for rating hiking trail difficulty. In fact, each system, park, guide, or hiker will give different information about trails. That depends on what a particular trail might be like for a subject, the weather, incline, etc.

In this book, I will use my own system for classifying trail difficulty, and I will also need to clarify what each of these cases is like. Regardless of whether we're talking about a beginner or intermediate hiker, every hiker will need to know what their hike is like before taking part in it. That is why I will set out this comprehensive description for each trail difficulty classification.

But what do I base this classification on? Well, after years of experience as a hiker, I will decide the difficulty based on certain factors. These factors include distance, elevation gain, and type of terrain. Therefore next, I will show you the beginner, intermediate, and advanced or expert hikes and their descriptions of what each of these hikes is like.

Beginner Hikes

Beginner hiking trails are an excellent way to introduce yourself and your family to the joys of hiking. These trails are designed for those with basic fitness levels and are suitable for most ages. These trails typically have a short duration of no more than two hours and a relatively flat and even terrain.

They are perfect for families with children or anyone who wants to take a leisurely stroll in the great outdoors. These trails often include interpretive signs, benches, and picnic areas for resting and relaxation along the way. They may also have amenities such as restrooms and drinking fountains.

Intermediate Hikes

Intermediate hiking trails are a step up from beginner trails, requiring more physical fitness and endurance. These trails are ideal for hikers with some experience and ready to take on longer and slightly more challenging hikes. They are typically characterized by a moderate incline and slightly uneven terrain, making them a good option for hikers who want to challenge themselves.

These hikes can take up to four and a half hours to complete with a longer distance compared to beginner trails. They're perfect for those who are reasonably fit and have some experience with hiking. Still, the trail can be challenging. There are some moderate inclines, rocky sections, and rough patches, but they're not as steep or as rugged as advanced trails.

Advanced/Expert Hikes

These are the most strenuous routes designed for seasoned hikers. These people have an appropriate fitness level and regularly hike. Advanced hikes can be tricky, so preparing for them is crucial.

That goes both mentally and physically. You will also need to have an understanding of the route and some hazards that you might come across. They're perfect for active and healthy adults and have steep, tricky terrain with numerous rocks, roots, and other obstacles.

These trails are more extended, demanding, and take more than five hours to complete with uneven terrain and significant elevation gain. You will also see steep inclines and declines and other challenges, so ensure you have all the appropriate gear, like hiking boots and trekking poles.

Your Top Banff Hiking Essentials

As you might know, Banff National Park is one of the best hiking locations worldwide. You can choose hikes according to your fitness level, ranging from extra easy to multi-day hikes. That is why there are some essentials you need while hiking here. These include:

Hiking Backpack

This piece of gear is needed when hiking because it helps you carry all the gear you need for your hike. As you know, you can't carry everything in your hands or around your waist. A backpack provides a convenient and comfortable way to carry everything you need!

A hiking backpack will have various features that will help you throughout your hike. First, the size is important because it should fit all the items you need for your hike. A bigger one can hold more items, but it could be heavier. A smaller one is perfect for shorter hikes but can't fit all the gear.

Your backpack should have a hip support feature that helps you distribute the weight across the hips and stops any strain on the shoulder and back regions. It should also have ventilation on the back to allow airflow throughout your body, keeping you cool and dry throughout the hike.

Your backpack should also have a hydration sleeve where you can fit your water bladder or bottle for easy access. It should also have multiple compartments and numerous pockets that will help you organize all the gear you have with you. You should also have a rain cover to protect your backpack and insides from any rain.

Bear Spray

Bear spray is there to defend you from bears during a hiking trip. They are generally afraid of humans and try to avoid any contact with them, but they can become angry and attack. That is why bear spray should always be near you! You can use it as a deterrent to scare the bear away and give you time to reach safety again.

How does bear spray work? It contains a chemical that irritates the bear's eyes, nose, and mouth and causes them to flee. Therefore, always carry bear spray with you when hiking in bear country because you will want to avoid any potential encounters.

Appropriate Footwear

Appropriate footwear is needed when hiking to protect your feet and provide comfort. Hiking involves walking long distances on uneven terrain, which can cause blisters, sore feet, and even injuries if you don't have the proper footwear. Good hiking shoes or boots have sturdy soles with good traction to prevent slips and falls.

You will also have added stability and support to your ankles and feet, which will help reduce the risk of any potential injuries. In the end, these boots are designed to be comfortable even while worn for an extended time frame. They should also allow you to focus on your hike instead of thinking about your feet all day.

Knife or Multi-tool

If you ask me, a knife or multi-tool is one of your first aid kit's most critical pieces of gear. It will come in handy for a variety of reasons and is used to cut ropes and sticks, roast marshmallows, or prepare food. Even in the case of an emergency, you can use it to cut bandages or clothing.

Additionally, it can help to fix gear or equipment, such as tightening loose screws on a backpack. Have a reliable and sharp knife or multi-tool with you while hiking, as it can be a versatile tool for a range of situations.

Water

When you hike, you are exposed to the sun and wind, which can cause dehydration and sunburn. By bringing enough water, you can stay hydrated and prevent heat exhaustion. But how much water is enough water for a hiker? It is recommended to bring at least 1 gallon of water per person a day, while strenuous hikes and longer or sunny days require more water.

Shelter

When hiking, it's important to have some form of shelter in case of unexpected weather changes or emergencies.

A shelter can provide protection from rain, wind, and cold temperatures. It can also provide a place to rest and recover in case of injury. Examples can be a bivy bag, hammock, or tent.

Rain Gear & Dry-Fast Layers

These pieces of gear are essential when hiking because weather conditions can change quickly and unexpectedly. If you get caught in the rain or encounter wet terrain, it can be uncomfortable and even dangerous if you get cold and wet.

Rain gear, such as a waterproof jacket and pants, will keep you dry and prevent hypothermia. Dry-fast layers such as quick-drying clothing and moisture-wicking socks will help regulate your body temperature and prevent blisters or other foot-related issues.

Sunscreen

Sunscreen is essential when hiking because it protects your skin from the sun's harmful UV rays, which can cause sunburn, skin damage, and even skin cancer. When you're out in the sun for an extended period of time, especially at high altitudes, apply sunscreen to all exposed areas of your skin to prevent damage.

Insect Repellent

It is also vital when hiking because it helps to keep away bugs such as mosquitoes and ticks that can carry diseases. Insects can be exceptionally bothersome in wooded areas or near bodies of water, so using insect repellent can help to prevent bites and the spread of diseases.

Garbage Bags

It's important to carry a garbage bag to avoid littering and to preserve the natural environment. You can pack your garbage, wrappers, food scraps, and other waste in a bag and dispose of it properly when you reach a garbage bin.

Whistle

It can be used to signal for help in case of an emergency or to alert others to your presence. If you get lost, injured, or stuck, you can use a whistle to make a loud noise which will help rescuers locate you. Whistles are lightweight and easy to carry, making them a simple yet effective tool for hikers.

High-Energy Hiking Food/Snacks

They provide the necessary fuel and nutrients to keep your body going during a long hike. Hiking is a physical activity that requires a lot of energy, so it's important to keep your body fueled with food that is high in protein, carbohydrates, and healthy fats. Examples of high-energy hiking food/snacks include trail mix, energy bars, nuts, and jerky.

Compass and Paper Map

Unlike electronic devices such as GPS, compasses and maps do not require batteries or an internet connection, making them reliable and useful tools outdoors. A compass helps you find your direction, and a paper map helps you understand the terrain and identify landmarks, such as peaks, rivers, and other features that can help you navigate. Ensure you know how to use them before setting out on your trail.

Hiking Etiquette

Just like any other sport, hiking has some rules too. Even though hiking isn't a competitive sport, there are still things we need to consider before we try out this pastime. While you discover new trails, live with nature, and spend time in your group, you will see how hiking is actually fun. It doesn't matter if you are hiking in a bigger group, with your pet, solo, or with your family. You will see that hiking difficulty and conditions will play a role in how you hike.

In fact, you will also see that hikers have a particular way of acting on the trail. It is called hiking etiquette, and these are the rules you have to know before you go hiking. Going unprepared and not knowing hiking rules will also lead to some weird stares, but it also could damage your safety. Therefore, I have prepared a few rules you need to follow before you head out on the trail. Here are some of the rules of hiking:

- **Prepare yourself:** Before going out on the trail, you must be informed about numerous things, like your route, conditions, weather forecast, maps, and park regulations. You will also need appropriate clothing, footwear, and gear.
- **Leave no trace:** While hiking, leave the trail and surroundings as you found them. So, pack out all the trash, bury human waste, and avoid damaging any plants, wildlife, and trails.
- **Stay on the trail:** Staying on designated trails helps to preserve the natural environment and avoid erosion or damage to vegetation. Wandering off the trail can be dangerous and increase the risk of getting lost.

- **Be kind to other hikers:** When encountering other hikers, be courteous and respectful. Yield to uphill hikers and stay to the right side of the trail. If you stop for a break, move to the side to allow others to pass.

- **Rules of passing by:** When passing another hiker, communicate your intention to pass with a friendly greeting or call out. Always pass on the left side and yield to the uphill hiker. Slow down and be cautious when passing, especially on narrow or steep sections of the trail.

- **Going to the bathroom:** When nature calls, hikers should always bury human waste at least 200 feet from water sources and trails. Hikers should also pack toilet paper or baby wipes in a plastic bag for disposal.

- **Hikers, mountain bikers, and riders:** Hikers should always yield to mountain bikers and horseback riders as they have less control over their speed and movement on the trail. Hikers should move off the trail on the downhill side to allow bikers or riders to pass safely.

- **Don't be too loud:** Be mindful of your noise level while on the trail. Loud noises and voices can disturb wildlife and other hikers' experiences. Hikers should also avoid using electronic devices with loudspeakers on the trail.

- **Mobile phones:** While having a mobile phone with you for emergencies is essential, hikers should keep it on silent mode to avoid disturbing the peace and tranquility of the trail. Additionally, hikers should avoid using their phones for non-emergency purposes while on the trail.

- **Hiking with a dog:** If you are hiking with your dog, keep them on a leash at all times to avoid disturbing wildlife and other humans.

Packing Checklist

Are you prepared to witness Banff's breathtaking scenery like never before? Although a picture can be visually appealing, there's something entirely different about confronting a mountain or trail head-on.

Photographs can't fully capture the incredible aspects of the great outdoors, such as the scent of nature, the gentle rustling of leaves in the wind, or the vivid hues surrounding you. They fail to do justice to the sweaty, heart-pumping sensation of the ascent or the overwhelming sense of gratitude and achievement once you've reached the summit. Stay tuned if you want a comprehensive packing checklist for Banff National Park, regardless of the season. Still, it is key to take some considerations in mind.

Therefore, the things you need to think about before visiting Banff are how accustomed you are to the cold and what season or weather type you will be visiting during. Before you pack your things, the first thing to do is check the weather for when you'll be visiting. It's not as easy as making a list for each season because there are six different types of weather here: a long winter, the time when winter changes to spring, spring, a short summer, fall, and the time when fall changes back into winter.

Another thing to consider when you pack is where you live. If you're not used to cold weather, except for some warmer summer days, you'll probably feel chilly most of the year in the mountains. Another thing to keep in mind is simple: What the dress code is?

When you're in Banff, you don't need to pack fancy clothes unless you're going to a wedding or other fancy event. The dress code is pretty casual. Even in restaurants at night, you can wear comfortable clothes like jeans. You don't need to pack high heels or a fancy dress.

But are there any special tips for hiking? Well, there are generalized tips I do need to point out, which you need to have in mind while packing:

- Wear the right shoes for the activities you have planned. Make sure they have good traction and are warm enough for the season. Don't forget to wear good socks too!
- Clothes made from special materials that can absorb sweat are better than cotton, which can stay wet and make you feel cold in chilly weather.
- Always carry extra clothes in a backpack when you're outdoors.
- Wear clothes in which you are comfortable, nothing too tight or too loose.
- Pack a small first aid kit, a compass, a pocketknife, and bear spray in your backpack, just in case!

Now that we have covered all the tips ensure you don't forget anything. For that, I am giving you a list of items you must have throughout the seasons and specialized gear for summer, winter, and mid-season.

All-Season Packing Checklist

Heading to Banff, but still trying to decide what to pack? If you love your multi-tool, this checklist is for you. Look no further than this all-season packing checklist. The unique climate Banff features, you have to make sure that you are prepared for any adventure that comes your way. Here are the essential items you need to have with you:

Essentials:

- ☐ Hiking backpack
- ☐ Bear spray
- ☐ Appropriate footwear
- ☐ Knife or Multi-Tool
- ☐ Water
- ☐ Shelter
- ☐ Rain Gear & Dry-Fast Layers
- ☐ Sunscreen
- ☐ Insect repellent
- ☐ Hiking first aid kit
- ☐ Garbage bags
- ☐ Whistle
- ☐ High-energy hiking food/snacks
- ☐ Compass and paper map

Clothing:

- ☐ Moisture-wicking underwear
- ☐ Hiking socks
- ☐ Moisture-wicking leggings
- ☐ Quick-drying pants
- ☐ Long sleeve moisture-wicking and UV protective shirt

- ☐ Sports bra
- ☐ Rain jacket
- ☐ Rain pants
- ☐ Thermal layers
- ☐ Hiking shoes OR hiking boots OR trail runners
- ☐ Gaiters
- ☐ Trekking poles
- ☐ Backpack rain cover

First Aid and Safety:

- ☐ First aid kit
- ☐ Multi-tool
- ☐ Sunscreen
- ☐ SPF lip balm
- ☐ Air horn
- ☐ Bear spray
- ☐ Insect repellent
- ☐ Sunglasses
- ☐ Matches
- ☐ Flashlight or headlamp
- ☐ Wallet
- ☐ Cash
- ☐ Credit card
- ☐ ID
- ☐ Insurance card
- ☐ GPS

- ☐ Permit
- ☐ Parking pass
- ☐ Phone
- ☐ Hiking app

Other:

- ☐ Trash bag
- ☐ Toilet paper
- ☐ Hand sanitizer
- ☐ Journal and pen
- ☐ Binoculars
- ☐ Energy bars
- ☐ Water bottle
- ☐ Hydration bladder
- ☐ Small water filtration system
- ☐ Ziplock bags
- ☐ Personal locator beacon
- ☐ Solar charger or Power bank

Get a backpack with padding and a buckle strap, hiking poles, and packing cubes to ensure comfort while hiking. Opt for quick-drying clothing, hiking socks, UV protective gear, and appropriate footwear. Bring microspikes or crampons for snowy terrain, rain gear, water shoes, and warm layers for cold weather. Protect yourself from danger with an air horn, knife, whistle, and first aid kit. Carry sunscreen, insect repellent, a map, compass, or GPS, and a flashlight. Bring cash, cards, and permits. Don't forget a journal, binoculars, and a trash bag to leave nature unspoiled.

Summer Packing Checklist

Finally, summer is near, but so are the bugs and crowds. If you're planning a trip to Banff in the summer, it's important to pack appropriately. Your gear should not be too warm to ensure you're comfortable and prepared for everything. This checklist includes items to help you stay cool, protected from the sun and insects, and comfortable while hiking or exploring the town. Here are the items I would recommend for summer hiking in Banff:

Essentials:

- ☐ Sandals
- ☐ Shorts
- ☐ Sun hat
- ☐ T-shirts
- ☐ Tank tops
- ☐ Windbreaker
- ☐ Bathing suit
- ☐ Don't forget:
- ☐ Sunglasses
- ☐ Sun protection
- ☐ Sunscreen
- ☐ Insect repellent

Winter Packing Checklist

Winter hiking is different from other hiking seasons. If you wish to scale the peaks, you will most often need some specialized gear. If you don't have any or the snow is deep, stick to easy hikes. Remember, winter in Banff can be harsh, with temperatures often dropping below freezing and high snowfall. I believe it's essential to pack appropriately for your visit, and here is what I bring:

Essentials:

☐ Waterproof jacket

☐ Waterproof pants

☐ Insulated footwear

☐ Base layers

☐ Mid-layers

☐ Gloves or mittens

☐ Face mask

☐ Neck gaiter

☐ Ski goggles

☐ Warm hat

☐ Hand warmers

Spring/Fall packing checklist

The mid or shoulder seasons in Banff are a bit tricky. The temperatures can fluctuate quite a bit during the day. It is important to pack a variety of layers to ensure that you are comfortable throughout your trip. But also, don't forget to check the weather report before leaving. Here are some essential items to consider when packing for spring and fall in Banff:

Essentials:

- Sunglasses
- T-shirts
- Windbreaker
- Base layers
- Mid-layers
- Rain gear

Conclusion

I hope you have learned how necessary preparation is for hiking. Don't forget that safety is your main concern, but also it rests upon some basics. These basics are learned and include planning, trail selection, and bringing all the recommended gear on your hike.

This chapter gave you all the safety information you needed as well as tips and included a few checklists that can help you hike. I hope you will use them before setting out to Banff National Park and that they prepare you for this adventure. Next, we will dive into the next chapter and cover the essential logistics all visitors need to know.

BANFF BASICS

I'm glad we have reached this chapter of our book! It's because this means that you have finally decided to actually visit this National Park. Needless to say, every visit anywhere needs to have some preparation.

In other words, you will need to know certain information that will get you there, help you stay, and enjoy your time. That is precisely why I am writing this chapter. It is there to tell you the basics about Banff National Park and give you anything you might need on your journey.

I will cover the essential logistics information which every visitor needs to know. They will have to plan their trip and include information like transportation options, accommodation, best visit times, and any potential passes and permits.

That doesn't just go for our national park but for any other national or nature park out there. You will need to know how to get there, where to stay, when to do it, and if any passes or permits are needed. It will help you have a safe and enjoyable experience and also help you choose the best time, accommodation, and transportation options to do so. It will educate you on any potential fees and permits you need to pay for before entering or enjoying the trails.

That is why you need to know some basics apart from the basics of hiking. I'm here to teach you the essential information about Canada's most stunning natural wonder, Banff. That is why, if you're planning a trip to Banff National Park, you're sure to have a fantastic experience. In fact, you will be surrounded by natural wonders, but you will also need to be prepared and understand the logistics and basics of the area.

Remember, preparation is key, and this needs to be done before embarking on your journey. But where can you start? Before doing anything, you need to know where and how to get there! I always remind everyone to check weather reports and trail conditions before heading out.

Also, choosing the right accommodation for your stay is crucial. Book accommodations in advance, especially during peak tourist seasons. Another crucial aspect to keep in mind is passes. Remember, obtaining the necessary permits and passes is vital. Activities, such as backcountry camping and fishing, require permits. That is why you need to remember these basics! By keeping them in mind, you'll be well-equipped to make the most of your time.

Best Time to Visit

Now, this is a tricky question to answer: When should one visit Banff? It depends on a lot of things! What do you want to do and experience during your trip? Choosing between a cold winter holiday and a warm one might be easy. Do you want to see mountains covered in snow or turquoise lakes? Do you like skiing or other winter sports or hiking in the backcountry? Or do you prefer taking casual walks or moderate hikes? Depending on your answers, you will have to choose your own time to visit.

If you ask me, Banff National Park is a stunning destination throughout the year. Just like any other park, each season offers different experiences and activities. When deciding which season to visit, consider the number of daylight hours. Keep in mind that it varies significantly between seasons.

During the summer months, one can enjoy water activities such as kayaking, canoeing, and paddleboarding. It is also the best time of year for hiking, camping, and other outdoor adventures.

If you're interested in wildlife viewing, I got you. Then, the best time to visit is during the autumn season as the temperatures cool down. The animals become more active and move closer to the roads and trails. If you also want to enjoy the fall leaves, consider visiting this time too. This is the time when the fall foliage is at its peak.

One can enjoy a true Christmas in the winter with snow-covered mountains and frozen lakes. One can participate in skiing, snowboarding, snowshoeing, and ice skating. Finally, spring is a quieter time to visit Banff. While some lakes may still be frozen, the warmer temperatures bring the mountains to life.

Ultimately, the best season to visit Banff National Park depends on your personal preferences. Decide or choose between water activities, wildlife viewing, fall foliage, or winter adventures; Banff has something to offer year-round; it is up to you.

Still, these are all the positive sides. As you might know, every season has its downsides. The winters in the mountains are long, so these parks are still covered in snow until April or May. Many people suggest visiting from late June to mid-September for hiking, scenery, and warmer weather. But during this time, there are lots of crowds, and prices for accommodation and airfare are very high.

If you want to save money and avoid crowds, consider going during the shoulder season, like mid-September to mid-October. That is my advice on deciding on a time to visit Banff. Next, we will explore the different time frames one can visit, when is the best time to visit if you are a hiker, and how long one needs to stay.

3 Seasons of Banff

What seasons are there in Banff? Which one should you choose? Rather than selecting a season to visit Banff National Park, choosing a time frame based on your desired activities may be more convenient. Read through the activities above and choose a time when to visit. The three seasons that you can visit here include winter, summer, and mid-season.

Winter: These activities usually occur from December to mid-April, while warmer weather activities extend from late spring through early fall. During winter, skiing is the primary activity. Other winter activities can include snowshoeing, ice skating, and sleigh rides are available as well. Non-skiing activities can continue through April, depending on the snow conditions and temperature.

Ski hills start opening some runs in mid-November and remain open until mid-May. December and the New Year's holiday can be very busy with high hotel prices. January and February can have very cold temperatures, but they host a variety of exciting festivals and events. In March and April, snow activities are still available, and temperatures are less likely to be extremely cold.

Mid-Season: Mid-April to mid-June and mid-October to November is known as the transition months when neither winter nor summer activities are available. These are considered the low season with reduced accommodation and airfare costs. It is an appropriate time for general sightseeing. However, you will see limited access to some parts, unpredictable weather, and frozen higher-elevation lakes.

Summer: Warmer weather activities usually begin from June to mid-October. Hiking, horseback riding, rafting, canoeing, fly fishing, and golfing are all possible from early June, and many campgrounds open in mid-to-late May. Most of these activities can be enjoyed through September, and some tourist attractions remain open until early to mid-October.

June is the wettest month here, but it is also an excellent time to view turquoise-colored lakes with snow-covered mountains. Early wildflowers can be seen in lower elevations, and it's an excellent opportunity to spot grizzly bears and other wildlife. The warmer temperatures make it the best time for hiking, with good access to all trails. Tourist attractions are still open, and the beautiful yellow colors of larch and aspen leaves appear in mid-to-late September.

When to Visit as a Hiker?

The ideal time for hiking in Banff National Park is from May to October, the prime hiking season. However, until the end of June, some mountain passes and trails at higher elevations may still be covered with snow, making them inaccessible. In June and July, the water flow in streams is at its highest, and some of the more remote trails that have few bridges require fording the streams.

Most hiking trails are accessible from late May to early October, except for those that are snowbound. Lower elevation trails are in a hotter climate, so they are the first to clear of snow, while higher sub-alpine and alpine ridge trails can remain snowbound through June and even into July.

Avalanches can be a danger! It goes from late winter through spring until early June. Trail conditions can be checked online through Parks Canada. September and early October are great for hiking, with blue skies, slightly cooler temperatures, and no mosquitoes. June is the start of mosquito season, and they can be a nuisance in forested areas and near lakes and wetlands. May and November are the least favorite times to visit the parks because of snow, wet and muddy areas, and uninspiring landscapes.

September and early October are our favorite times of the year because of the larch and aspen trees' beautiful yellow and gold colors. The crowds are smaller than in summer, and the temperatures are perfect for hiking. There are usually no mosquitoes, and hotel prices and airfares are more favorable than in July and August.

Remember, regardless of the month; it's important to plan your hiking trips according to your skill level and the weather conditions and to always check the trail conditions and forecasts before heading out. It's also recommended to hike with a partner or group and to let someone know your itinerary before starting your hike.

How Long to Stay?

The ideal length of stay in Banff National Park depends on your interests and the activities you want to engage in. Most importantly, it also depends on the amount of free time you have booked. Therefore, in the best case, I would stay two weeks, but if you don't have that much time, the least amount is three days.

If you have two weeks, you can truly immerse yourself in the local culture. Beyond the famous Lake Louise, there are many other turquoise-hued lakes to explore, such as Two Jack, Bow, Hector, Johnson, and Herbert Lakes. You can also go beyond the popular Cascade and Rundle peaks for hiking and try lesser-known mountains like Hector, Bourgeau, and Forbes. Take your time and plan ahead. With two weeks, you have the chance to revisit your favorite places and activities, indulge in downtime, and truly connect with the beauty of the area.

For a one-week stay, you can still experience much of what Banff National Park has to offer. With over 200 trails, you can choose to take a simple stroll or embark on more challenging hikes. Make sure to leave time for exploring canyons, tea houses, and waterfalls, and enjoy some leisurely activities such as sightseeing and golfing. You can also fit in a tour or two, such as a horseback adventure or a self-guided art and museum exploration.

With just five days, you can still tick off some of the must-see spots in Banff and Lake Louise. Dedicate a day to the Lake Louise region and another to the Banff townsite and choose a tour that matches your interests.

If you only have three days, choose the experiences that matter most to you. A visit to Lake Louise and Johnston Canyon is a must, and Tunnel Mountain is an easy win for hiking with breathtaking views. In the end, no matter how much time you have in Banff National Park, you're sure to be enchanted by the mountains and promise to return.

Restrictions and Closures

Like every other park, Banff occasionally has some restrictions for driving and presents closures in certain areas, usually due to weather or other natural phenomena. These are subject to changes depending on the weather and snow conditions and can be lifted.

- Bow Valley Parkway: No vehicle, bicycle, or foot access is allowed from 8 p.m. to 8 a.m. March to June.
- Moraine Lake Road: Starting 2023 this road is closed to all personal vehicle traffic.
- Icefields Parkway: Temporary closures can last for several days due to heavy snowfall or avalanches.
- Lake Minnewanka Loop: This road is closed from November to May.

No facilities or fuel are available on these trails from November to the end of March. Due to the snow, most natural attractions are hard to access. Make sure you check the info on the official site before heading off!

How to Get to Banff National Park

Transportation options and getting there are vital elements in any trip. If you ask me, it doesn't matter how you get there. The main deal is that you're out in nature. Still, if Banff is quite a distance away from your current location, it might be wise to plan in advance.

Use planes, trains, buses, and automobiles to get here, but the choice of transportation mode depends on you. If you prefer a more leisurely pace and enjoy driving, then taking a road trip is a great option. Calgary International Airport is the closest airport to Banff National Park. It is approximately 1.5 hours away by car. Alternatively, you could take a train or bus.

Flying

What is the quickest and most direct way to reach Banff National Park? Well, flying, of course. And the nearest major airport to Banff is the Calgary International Airport.

Many airlines operate flights to Calgary International Airport, which is the primary gateway to Banff and Lake Louise. To get from the airport to Banff, you will need less than 2 hours. You will need approximately 40 minutes to drive from Banff to get to Lake Louise. Visitors can book vehicle rentals for pick-up at the airport or choose one of the frequent shuttle services.

If you are flying into Vancouver International Airport, choose your transportation. You can take a bus, train, or rent a car to reach Banff National Park, which is approximately 850 km (530 miles) away. Rider Express offers an affordable bus service, but it can take up to 15 hours and includes 13 stops.

Edmonton International Airport is another airport near Banff National Park, located about 360 km (224 miles) north of the park. Driving to the park from the airport takes about 3 hours and 30 minutes. However, most visitors coming from outside Canada prefer to fly into either Calgary or Edmonton International Airport. You can book vehicles for pick-up and drop-off at the airport or use shuttle services to reach Jasper.

If you ask me, flying into Calgary or Edmonton airports is the best option. That is because driving from Vancouver to the Rockies is not recommended during the early spring and winter. Snowstorms or avalanches can cause temporary road closures or delays.

Shuttle Service

Another valuable option for reaching Banff is a shuttle from the airport. Banff Airporter provides shuttle services from the airport to Banff National Park. You can book your space with them.

With Banff Airporter, you can ride a comfortable shuttle bus from Calgary Airport to Canmore (1 hour and 20 minutes) or Banff (2 hours).

Banff Airporter offers different pricing options that depend on the number of people in your group and whether you need round-trip transportation. The shuttle seats are comfortable; the best part is you don't have to drive. You can relax, enjoy the views, charge your phone, or even take a nap to recharge yourself!

Bus Service

Guided tours to the Rocky Mountains are available from various companies in Vancouver, which include scenic stops and activity options. Such tours are a good option for those unable to drive, but their fixed schedules and short time at each location can be limiting. Certain companies such as Brewster Tours, Timberwolf Tours, West Trek Tours, and Moose Travel provide tours that cater to various budgets.

Rider Express Transportation now offers services from Calgary and Vancouver. Alternatively, the On-It Transit service provides direct transportation from Calgary to Banff. Do so for $10 CAD ($7.40 USD) each way, available on weekends and some holidays from mid-May to mid-September. However, reservations are required, and the service does not operate from the airport.

Train

Train travel is not as economical in Canada as it is in other places. Two train companies offer service to the Rocky Mountains. Via Rail operates twice a week between Vancouver and Jasper from May through October. You can continue your journey on Via Rail to other cities across Canada, all the way to Halifax.

Tickets should be booked early for the best pricing, but you miss out on some scenery as the train runs overnight. You can select from a standard seat or pay an additional fee for a sleeping compartment, but there's no regular train service for passengers to Banff.

A posh train service, Rocky Mountaineer, is available between late April and early October. Unlike Via Rail, it only operates during the day so travelers can appreciate the stunning landscapes. The train travels from Vancouver to Banff or Jasper, and there are also alternatives that link Whistler to Jasper. There is no sleeping accommodation available on the train, and nights are spent in hotels as part of a package deal.

Trains don't take passengers to places like the Icefields Parkway, so combining train travel with other transportation options is recommended. This train offers a two-day trip from Vancouver to Banff with stops in Lake Louise and Banff, services running from mid-April to mid-October. If you can afford the time and price, this luxurious travel option will create memories that will last a lifetime.

Driving

Banff National Park is located beside the TransCanada Highway, which is the main road that goes across Canada and is open all year round. This highway has four lanes and goes through the middle of Banff National Park.

If you are coming from Calgary in the east, the main entrance gates to Banff National Park are about a 1 hour and 15-minute drive (125 km or 77 miles) away. If you are coming from Vancouver in the west, Banff National Park is a day's drive (850 km or 530 miles) away. You will drive through the

Coast Mountains, British Columbia's wine country, and the Canadian Rockies.

If you are coming from the Edmonton area, you can take AB-2 South. It will lead you to the Trans-Canada Highway, which leads to Calgary and then continues west to the park. If you are coming from the south, cities in the United States, like Kalispell, Montana, are just over 5 hours away (480 km or 300 miles).

When planning to drive here, you should think about the road conditions throughout the year. Some roads are open during the winter, but driving on snowy or icy roads can be dangerous. These conditions are common in the higher elevations in November through April and into May.

When driving from Vancouver to Calgary or vice versa, you should include the Icefields Parkway in your itinerary. It has impressive views and is considered one of the top drives in North America. The most common and quickest route is Vancouver – Jasper – Icefields Parkway – Lake Louise – Banff – Calgary or vice versa.

What about car rentals? Rental companies usually charge a one-way drop-off fee that can be as much as $1000 on top of the rental costs. Finding a cheap flight between Calgary and Vancouver may be cheaper than renting a car to tour each place. Or you can fly in and out of the same airport and drive in a circle between the west coast and the mountains.

Some people prefer traveling by motorhome or camper van to and/or around the mountains. You can rent an RV to drive from Vancouver to the mountains or rent one in Calgary for touring around the mountains. However, it can be expensive to travel this way in Canada. A basic RV rental costs around $1500 a week, and you also have to pay for bed linens, dishes, insurance, fuel costs, and campground fees.

Travel in the Banff Region

Walking is the most recommended way to navigate Banff, but in cases of unfavorable weather, this quaint resort town provides a user-friendly bus system. Additionally, many hotels offer a complimentary shuttle that services both the town and skiing areas, and all three ski hills also provide complimentary shuttles between the hills and the town.

The town's "Roam" bus system offers convenient transportation to various points of interest. However, the buses' schedules are sporadic, so it's best to check the town's public transit website for specific routes and timetables.

For adults, the fare for rides within Banff costs $2 CAD (about $1.50), seniors and kids pay $1 CAD (or approximately $0.80), and children under six ride for free. An unlimited day pass can also be purchased for $5 CAD (or about $4), and the service operates daily from 6:15 a.m. to 11:30 p.m.

Directions to Banff National Park, Alberta

It is effortless to travel by car from Calgary to Banff, as the 90-minute drive from Calgary Airport to Banff is mostly on freeways or highways, with minimal city driving involved, providing picturesque views throughout the journey.

If you choose to drive from Edmonton to Banff, the drive can be relatively dull unless you opt for the longer route through Jasper National Park, followed by the Icefields Parkway, which is recognized as one of the most beautiful drives worldwide. However, this will increase the driving time to approximately 7.5 hours.

The drive from Kelowna or Vancouver to Banff is breathtaking, with the majority of the route going through mountainous terrain. Depending on the path you take, you'll experience scenic views from the Coast Mountains, Colombia Mountains, and the Canadian Rocky Mountains.

Accommodations and Lodging Options

Checking out all the Banff restaurants in just a single-day trip is impossible. Luckily, a wide variety of exceptional hotels and accommodations is available here. Banff, a bustling town, and Lake Louise, a serene village, will cater to every traveler's preferences.

You can opt for lavish hotels, family-friendly chalets, cozy beds and breakfasts, or economical hostels. You could also enjoy several campgrounds and RV sites, but for the ultimate alpine getaway, you can trek on foot or ski to a remote backcountry lodge.

If you are planning an extended stay in Banff, selecting the right hotel, hostel, or campground is vital. To assist you in your search, I've compiled a list of my preferred places to stay. These are the stays I would recommend for you:

Cabin - Banff Log Cabin

Stay in the Banff Log Cabin Guesthouse, a romantic and unique cabin that can accommodate a maximum of 2 people. It is located in the heart of the Canadian Rocky Mountains, just a short 4-minute walk from the Fairmont Banff Springs Hotel and a 5-minute drive from the world-class Banff Springs Golf Course.

The cabin is located in an exclusive residential area on a quiet street, providing off-street parking. It has modern amenities with a rustic ambiance and is separate from the main house, ensuring complete privacy. It's perfect for a romantic getaway, weekend retreat, or honeymoon vacation.

- Offering: 2 people
- Minimal stay: None
- Reservation: Yes, it can be canceled
- Dogs: No
- Wi-Fi: Yes
- Food on site: Yes
- Free parking: Yes
- Toilet: Yes

Pros:

- Private
- Clean

Cons:

- Pricy
- Often booked out

Hotels and Inns - Emerald Lake Lodge

Emerald Lake Lodge is a historic property, built in 1902 by the Canadian Pacific Railway, which sits on the secluded Emerald Lake, surrounded by the breathtaking Rocky Mountains. The lodge has 85 units in 24 chalet-style cabins, all featuring cozy duvets, wood-burning fireplaces, and balconies or patios with magnificent views.

The lodge also offers a comfortable lounge, bar, and a snooker table, where casual fare is served. During winter, enjoy excellent cross-country skiing trails and snowshoeing opportunities. During summer, go canoeing on the lake and hiking on the lodge's grounds. It is perfect for those seeking a romantic, relaxing getaway in the Rockies.

- Minimal stay: None
- Reservation: Yes, it can be canceled
- Dogs: No
- Wi-Fi: Yes
- Food on site: Yes
- Free parking: Yes
- Toilet: Yes

Pros:

- Amazing location
- Secluded

Cons:

- Far away
- Often booked out

Bed and Breakfasts - Beaujolais Boutique B&B At Thea's House

Thea's house is a special place that combines the charm of a bed & breakfast with the modern comforts of a boutique hotel. I love it because it shows the hospitality of Banff and its people. It lies inside the town of Banff and offers cozy and private rooms with king-size beds, gas fireplaces, and cable TV.

Most visitors comment on the stunning mountain views from a small balcony. You can also enjoy delicious dinners from our award-winning restaurant, Le Beaujolais, without leaving the property. The whole place is entirely smoke-free and perfect for a romantic and relaxing getaway.

- Minimal stay: None
- Reservation: Yes, it can be canceled
- Dogs: No
- Wi-Fi: Yes
- Food on site: Yes

- Free parking: Yes
- Toilet: Yes

Pros:

- Great view

Cons:

- Pricy

Backcountry Lodges - Sundance Lodge

Sundance Lodge is a great place to escape from everyday life. The cozy log cabin lodge has ten rooms and is surrounded by thick woods, making it feel remote and secluded despite being only 16 km (10 miles) from Banff. The lodge is powered by solar power and wood heat and offers indoor washrooms, hot showers, and comfortable beds.

In winter, from January to March, visitors can snowshoe, fat bike, or cross-country ski on a 12 km trail from the Healy Creek Trailhead near Banff and stay overnight. The lodge is perfect for groups of friends or family who want to enjoy the place to themselves. In summer, the lodge is a resting place for riders on a multi-day horseback adventure.

- Minimal stay: None
- Reservation: Yes, it can be canceled
- Dogs: No
- Wi-Fi: Yes
- Food on site: Yes

- Free parking: Yes
- Toilet: Yes

Pros:

- Peaceful

Cons:

- Located in the backcountry

Basic and Hostels - The Dorothy Motel

The Dorothy Motel is a new boutique hotel in Banff that opened in 2020. It has modern rooms with 1 King or 2 Queen bed options and is located near Banff Avenue. The rooms have a mini-fridge, microwave, and coffee maker to help guests get ready for the day. Suppose guests have problems with their bikes while out on the trails; the motel has an on-site bike repair/maintenance station. The motel is pet-friendly by request and is located near Cascade Mountain.

- Minimal stay: None
- Reservation: Yes, it can be canceled
- Dogs: No
- Wi-Fi: Yes
- Food on site: Yes
- Free parking: Yes
- Toilet: Yes

Pros:

- Clean
- Cheap

Cons:

- Busy area

Camping

Camping in a tent is the most popular way to camp in Banff. It's easy if you have the right gear. To ensure you have a spot to camp, reserve a campsite before your trip. I suggest trying different campsites to see more of the park during your trip.

To make sure you're ready for your camping trip, bring warm clothes, waterproof clothing, hats and mitts, an umbrella, a groundsheet for your tent, a sleeping mat, a warm sleeping bag, and extra blankets. Remember that only a maximum of six people (including children) is allowed on each campsite, and the number of vehicles and tents allowed varies by campground.

When you arrive, check-in time is between 2 p.m. and 8 p.m. (3 p.m. to 8 p.m. for oTENTiks and Equipped camping), and check-out or re-registration is by 11 a.m. Payment can be made by card or cash. You can't use debit for self-registration campsites, so bring exact change or a credit card.

There is no Wi-Fi in the campgrounds, and you can only stay for a maximum of 14 nights. You must camp in a designated campground and site, and vehicles, trailers, and tents must be set up on the gravel or paved area. To camp in Banff National Park, you'll need a National Park Entry Pass, a camping permit, and a fire permit if you want to have a fire.

When washing dishes, use the outdoor sink or a personal basin, not the sinks inside the bathrooms. Dump dishwater down outdoor sinks or at the sani-dump in campgrounds. Recyclable bottles and cans can be recycled in each campground.

If you have children, please supervise them at all times to ensure their safety, and drive slowly and carefully in the campground. Remember to use roadways and pathways to access facilities, and always keep your pets on a leash.

Where to Camp

Next up, we will cover the numerous campsites one can use here, together with their amenities, offers and other information you might need:

Tunnel Mountain Village I

This is a popular campsite in Banff National Park, located near the town center. It is open from June to October and has 618 sites available for camping with tents or RVs. The amenities include toilets, showers with hot water, and fire pits. It's a good choice for first-time campers because it has everything you need, and the forested area protects you from the wind. The views of the nearby mountains are beautiful.

- Sites: 618
- Open dates: Jun-Oct
- Amenities: Hot water, fire pits, showers, dump station

- Camping type: Tent and RV
- Pets: Yes
- Toilet: Yes

Tunnel Mountain Village II

This is the only campground in Banff that is open year-round and close to the town. It has 188 sites available for camping with tents or RVs, with amenities such as electrical hookups, flush toilets, hot and cold showers, and fire pits. Most of the spaces are designed for RVs, but over 30 tent camping spots are also available.

- Sites: 188
- Open dates: All year
- Amenities: Hot water, fire pits, showers, hookups, dump station
- Camping type: Tent and RV
- Pets: Yes
- Toilet: Yes

Two Jack Main

Two Jack Main is a campsite close to Two Jack Lake, Lake Minnewanka, and Mount Rundle. It has over 300 campsites, fire pits, and running water. But you won't be able to take a hot shower here.

- Sites: 300
- Open dates: Jun-Sept
- Amenities: Shelters, firepits, dump station

- Camping type: Tent and RV
- Pets: Yes
- Toilet: Yes

Two Jack Lakeside

This is my top pick for a campground in Banff National Park. It's a smaller campground with only 64 spots and only for people camping in tents. But the views of Mount Rundle reflecting on the lake are breathtaking. You'll wake up to beautiful views of the mountains and hear the sounds of birds. And, on clear nights, you can see the stars above the trees. It's the perfect spot for a picturesque camping experience in Banff National Park.

- Sites: 64
- Open dates: May-Oct
- Amenities: Shelters, firepits, dump station, showers
- Camping type: Tent and RV
- Pets: Yes
- Toilet: Yes

Johnston Canyon Campground

The Johnston Canyon campground is only 25 km away from Banff town and is a great option for people who want a more natural camping experience. You can set up a tent or park a small RV there. The campground is close to the popular Johnston Canyon Trail, and you can catch a bus to Banff during the summer.

- Sites: 132
- Open dates: Dependable
- Amenities: Shelters, firepits, dump station, showers
- Camping type: Tent and RV
- Pets: Yes
- Toilet: Yes

Castle Mountain Campground

This is small and cozy, with no fancy services. It's located in a forested area along Bow Valley Parkway and only 32 km from Banff town. You can park a small RV or set up a tent there. There are nearby attractions, such as Silverton Falls and Johnston Canyon. The campground operates on a first-come, first-served basis, and you can pay with cash or credit card.

- Sites: 43
- Open dates: Dependable
- Amenities: Shelters, firepits
- Camping type: Tent and RV
- Pets: Yes
- Toilet: Yes

Protection Mountain Campground

It is situated 15 km east of Lake Louise on the Bow Valley Parkway. You'll get stunning views of Protection and Castle Mountains and can enjoy a sky full of stars at night. You can catch Roam Public Transit to Banff or Lake Louise, so you won't have to worry about parking. RV campers can use the sani-dump at Lake Louise Campground. There's limited cell coverage in the area. Castle Mountain is a first-come, first-served campsite, which means you can't book it in advance. You'll need to give your credit card number or cash when you arrive. It's an excellent option for those who don't want to make reservations.

- Sites: 72
- Open dates: Jun-Sept
- Amenities: Shelters, firepits
- Camping type: Tent and RV
- Pets: Yes
- Toilet: Yes

Lake Louise

Book the Lake Louise campground in advance for a great camping spot near Lake Louise. It's just 1 kilometer away from Lake Louise, with nearby hikes and views. The campground has all the necessary amenities and is suited for tents, tent trailers, or small motorhomes and trailers up to 7 meters. There are fire and no-fire loops for group camping. The forested campground is divided into two sections: hard-sided and soft-sided camping. An electric fence encloses the soft-sided area and allows tents and soft-sided trailers. The hard-sided area is for hard-sided camping units only.

- Sites: 189 + 206
- Open dates: May-Sept
- Amenities: Shower, shelters, firepits, electricity, dump station

- Camping type: Tent and RV
- Pets: Yes
- Toilet: Yes

Mosquito Creek

This is a campground that's open from May 31 to October 14, with 32 campsites available for tents and RVs. There are dry toilets and fire pits, and the location is excellent for hikes and views in the Columbia Icefield area. Despite its name, mosquitos aren't a big problem here. The campsite is first-come, first-served, and it's on the Icefields Parkway, which gives you access to many hikes in Jasper and the surrounding areas.

- Sites: 32
- Open dates: May-Sept
- Amenities: Firepits, shelter
- Camping type: Tent
- Pets: Yes
- Toilet: Yes, outhouse

Silverhorn Creek

Silverhorn Creek is another first-come, first-served campground on the Icefields Parkway. It has 45 campsites for tents and RVs, dry toilets, and fire pits. It's more primitive, with no running water, but it has great views of the Columbia Icefield area.

- Sites: 45
- Open dates: May-Sept

- Amenities: Firepits, shelter
- Camping type: Tent
- Pets: Yes
- Toilet: Yes, outhouse

Rampart Creek

This is the last Icefields Parkway campground and has primitive facilities, offering only dry toilets and fire pits. It is also a first-come, first-served campground.

- Sites: 51
- Open dates: May-Oct
- Amenities: Firepits, shelter
- Camping type: Tent
- Pets: Yes
- Toilet: Yes, outhouse

Waterfowl Lakes

This is a very popular campground in Banff with the largest number of campsites. Although no shower facilities exist, it is the only Icefields Parkway campground with running water. This wooded campground welcomes both tents and campervans and offers flush toilets and fire pits.

- Sites: 110
- Open dates: May-Sept
- Amenities: Firepits, shelter
- Camping type: Tent

- Pets: Yes
- Toilet: Yes

Backcountry Camping

If you're an outdoor enthusiast, you can try backcountry camping in Banff National Park. That means hiking with all your gear and camping in a designated area off the hiking trail. Backcountry campsites offer great views, but you need a permit to camp in the backcountry, which you can purchase in advance.

There are limited permits, so book early, and it can be obtained online or by phone. You must have a copy of the permit with you and show it to Parks Canada staff when asked. Reservations are necessary, and a fee is charged. Finally, don't forget you need a National Park Pass to enter the park.

You must also plan your trekking route before you go since there are specifically designated areas for camping. Parks Canada provides hiking route suggestions on their website. Be sure to have all the necessary camping gear and a thoroughly mapped-out route before heading out.

There may be fewer maintained trails in remote areas of the park, so be prepared to be self-reliant. When camping, make sure to camp at least 5 km away from any campground or trailhead and set up your tent at least 50 m from the trail and 70 m from water sources. Cook and store your food away from your tent and use bear-resistant food containers between April and November. Remember to bring a stove, as fires are not allowed in random camping areas.

But when is the best time to camp in the backcountry? July and August are the best months for hiking in the backcountry of Banff National Park, but even in summer, snow can be found at higher elevations. September is usually drier but colder and more likely to have snow.

It's important to be aware of natural hazards and have wilderness first aid training when planning a backcountry trip. Plan ahead to minimize risks and check current trail conditions, warnings, and closures at a Parks Canada visitor center.

Make sure you have enough food, water, clothing, and equipment for your trip. Have bear spray, a first aid kit, and a satellite emergency communication device. Let someone know where you're going and when you'll be back. Ticks carrying Lyme disease may be present in the park, so check yourself and your pet after hiking. Be alert for wildlife and avoid wearing earbuds or headphones. Some of the backcountry campsites in the area include:

- Egypt Lake (E13)
- Baker Lake (Sk11)
- Merlin Meadows (Sk18)
- Aylmer Pass Junction (Lm8)
- Howard Douglas Lake (Su8)
- Marvel Lake (Br13)
- McBride's Camp (Br14)
- Ball Pass Junction (Re21)
- Twin Lakes (Tw7)
- Aylmer Canyon (Lm9)

- Mt. Inglismaldie (Lm11)
- Glacier Lake (Gl9)

Equipped Campsites

Never tried camping and don't want to invest in the gear? At Banff National Park, there are two pre-equipped campsites at Two Jack Main Campground, which are perfect for people who don't have their own camping gear or don't want the hassle of packing everything. Each site includes a 6-person canvas tent set up on a wooden platform, sleeping cots, a stove, and a bear-proof food locker. However, you need to bring your own personal items like a sleeping bag, pillow, flashlight, kitchen gear, clothes, and other essential items.

Still, some rules need to be followed: you must store all food and related items in your vehicle or wildlife-proof locker. You're not allowed to eat or drink inside the tent, smoke, or bring pets in. Also, it's important to keep in mind that you need a reservation confirmation number before leaving!

- Sites: 32
- Open dates: May-Sept
- Amenities: Firepits, shelter, shower,
- Camping type: Tent
- Pets: Yes
- Toilet: Yes

oTENTik

Another great idea is the oTENTik tents, which require no setup, similar to glamping. Parks Canada has a special type of accommodation called oTENTik, which is a mix of a cabin and a tent. They are complete with raised floors, cozy beds, and furniture for a comfortable stay in the wild. Ideal for families and friends of all ages.

What's included in your stay? Standard amenities include space for 5-6 people, 3-5 mattresses, an indoor table with bench or chairs, and lighting powered by electricity, solar, or batteries. Your site may also come with additional features such as a USB port, heating (in most units), a deck with outdoor furniture, a cook shelter, a barbecue, and a fire pit.

You'll need to pack bedding and pillows, a flashlight, a lantern, or a headlamp—personal gear like clothing, accessories, and toiletries. Personal safety items include a whistle, first aid kit, sunscreen, bug repellent, cooking equipment (ask when you reserve), food and drinks, reusable water bottles, entertainment items, other essentials like matches or a lighter, and rope. Check out our camping checklist or download the Parks Canada App to edit and save your packing list.

Two Jack Lakeside oTENTik

This location features 10 oTENTiks, so if you want to camp on the peaceful shores of Two Jack Lake, surrounded by trees, this is the place for you. It's a great starting point for outdoor activities like hiking and canoeing.

- Sites: 10
- Open dates: May-Oct
- Amenities: Firepits, shelter, shower, electricity,

- Camping type: oTENTik tent
- Pets: Yes
- Toilet: Yes

Tunnel Mtn. Village II oTENTik

It has 21 oTENTiks that provide a cozy and intimate camping experience, and it's located close to town and hiking and biking trails.

- Sites: 21
- Open dates: May-Oct
- Amenities: Firepits, shelter, shower, electricity,
- Camping type: oTENTik tent
- Pets: Yes
- Toilet: Yes

Required Passes

All National Parks of Canada visitors must have a Canada National Park Day Pass, or an annual pass called the Discovery Pass. Why would you need to pay this? I understand that some people might be against paying for nature. Believe me, it's worth it!

Entry and service fees help maintain visitor services and facilities. Every time you visit, you're investing in the park and leaving a legacy for future generations. If you want your children and their children to enjoy nature the way it is now, you need to pay for your pass.

The Canadian Rockies have four parks: Banff National Park, Kootenay National Park, Yoho National Park, and Jasper National Park. Although there's no official "Banff Park Pass," you can purchase day passes for the parks of the Canadian Rockies or a Parks Canada annual pass that works in all National Parks in Canada.

Do you need a Banff Park Pass?

The entry fees for the Canadian National Parks in the Rocky Mountains can be confusing. It's not a flat fee! Only pay for the number of days you will be in the parks. The pass is associated with the vehicle entering the parks, but the charge is determined on a per-passenger basis. You'll receive one pass per vehicle, and it should be placed on the dashboard or hung from the rearview mirror.

To enter Banff National Park and the surrounding parks, all visitors must have a park pass regardless of their mode of transportation. There is no specific "Banff Park Pass," but rather a Canada National Park Pass that includes all national parks in the country.

Even if you are just visiting for the day, you must still obtain a Park Pass. The fees collected for Park Passes are used to support visitor services and facilities in the park.

You are not required to have a pass if you are driving through Banff National Park via TransCanada. But you must have a pass if you want to stop at any scenic spots or hiking trails. Passes are also needed for scenic drives on the Icefields Parkway (93) and Bow Valley Parkway (1A).

You must have a valid park pass if you plan to visit a national park by car or rented vehicle. The same goes for those arriving by bus or shuttle and renting a vehicle inside the park. It is required to purchase a park pass for yourself and all your passengers for each day you'll be in the park. If you're joining a tour operator, you should confirm with them if they will provide the park pass for you.

Some visitors mistakenly believe they don't need a pass for short stops in places like the town of Banff or for a quick meal during their drive. However, a park pass is required for stopping at viewpoints or pullouts to take photos, visiting Lake Louise, using picnic areas, attending events or festivals in the park (for personal or business purposes), stopping in towns or villages like the Banff town site, camping, hiking, using park facilities, or skiing for the day.

But where can you get these passes? You can buy Park Passes in three ways: online, at the park gates (if you are driving to Banff National Park), or in person at the Visitor Center located in Banff and Lake Louise.

Banff Park Pass options

Visitors can choose between daily or annual fees when purchasing a Canada National Park Pass. Buying an annual pass, also known as the Discovery Pass, is a better value if you plan to spend seven or more days in the parks. However, if you only need access for a single day, you can purchase a daily pass for either an individual or a family.

Day passes grant visitors access to Banff and other parks. They are valid until 4:00 p.m. on the day following purchase and can be bought online or in person at specific locations.

The Discovery Pass provides access to all the National Parks of Canada, as well as many National Sites, and there is no park-specific annual pass available for the Canadian Rockies parks like Banff or Jasper.

It is the recommended choice for most visitors, as it offers admission to all national parks and sites operated by Parks Canada for an entire year. Suppose you're only visiting the Rocky Mountain parks. In that case, a day pass will grant you entry to the region's Banff, Jasper, Yoho, Kootenay, Waterton, Elk Island, Revelstoke, and Glacier National Parks. Now that we have that covered, these are the prices:

Daily	Prices as of 2023 (CAD)
Adult	$ 10.50
Senior	$ 9.00
Family/Group	$ 21.00
Commercial Group, per person	$ 9.00
Youths below 17 years	Free
Parks Canada Discovery Pass	
Adult	$ 72.25
Senior	$ 61.75
Family/Group	$ 145.25

Wi-Fi and Cellular Access

All hikers know that cell phone service can be unreliable in the mountains. That is why you can only sometimes count on having cell phone service while hiking. In most cases, you have service in towns and hotels, but not in some parts of the parks.

If you do not have a plan that includes Canada, you can get charged a lot for using your phone. That goes even if you do not use your phone, so turn off data on your phone before coming to Canada. Also, use a GPS app that does not need data. One can also get a free local map from the tourist center.

Only use the internet when you are connected to Wi-Fi. In Banff, you can usually get free Wi-Fi at hotels, coffee shops, pubs, and restaurants, but it is harder to find outside of town. In Lake Louise, free Wi-Fi is not easy to find and may not be very good.

Conclusion

I hope you understand the potential visiting times, permits, accommodation, getting there, and communication options in Banff National Park. When planning a trip, be well-prepared and have all the necessary information beforehand. If you wish to have an unforgettable and hassle-free experience in this breathtaking natural wonder, make sure you have all the information you need. Therefore, use this chapter, or this book, as a guide.

It doesn't matter if it's choosing the ideal accommodation to transportation options, from required passes and permits to the best time to visit. This section covers everything that you need to know. It's everything you need to get you hiking. Next, we will explore beginner hikes, so stay tuned.

FINDING YOUR FOOTING

Finally, we arrived at the most important destination of our journey. The goal of this book was to showcase the best hikes of Banff National Park, and if you have reached this chapter right here, you're probably already planning your trip. Lucky you!

Now, if you want to imagine what this national park is like, imagine that you're stepping into a beautiful world where you will see towering cliffs, crystal-clear water, and lush forests. They surround you and make you feel like you're in a fairy tale. Now, the goal of this chapter is to take you on a journey through some of the best beginner hikes in Banff. We will explore the best beginner hikes in this national park, which include Johnston Canyon, Lake Louise, Rockpile, and Fenland Trail, so stay tuned to learn more about them.

Johnston Canyon to Upper Falls

The hike through Johnston Canyon in Banff National Park is a gorgeous walk through a narrow canyon with close-up views of Johnston Creek before it meets the Bow River. Expect crowds, as this is a very popular and easy hike on a unique trail in Banff National Park. The trail is open year-round, so if crowds bother you, consider visiting in the winter.

Johnston Canyon is named after a man who found gold in the creek in 1910. Even though you won't find gold on your walk, you'll see beautiful turquoise water beneath golden canyon walls covered in tall evergreen trees. The colors on this hike are stunning. As you walk on the catwalk high above the water, you can enjoy the sights and listen to the peaceful sound of the babbling creek and the occasional roar of the falls echoing off the canyon walls.

The well-maintained catwalk trail provides excellent views of the bright blue creek below as it cascades down seven waterfalls. There are several viewpoints at each waterfall, and even a tunnel in the cliff that adds to the hike's uniqueness. This hike is a must-do for anyone visiting Banff National Park.

The lower falls viewing area has a high overlook, a lower bridge, and a short rock tunnel that leads to a misty view at the base of the falls. The upper falls area is just as exciting, with a lower catwalk that sits right above the water and a high viewpoint on top of the cliff.

The trail starts in a developed area with a large parking lot and restrooms near Johnston Canyon Resort, founded by Walter and Marguerite Camp in 1927. The Camps were responsible for constructing the trail through the canyon with funding from Banff National Park. The Camp family still runs the resort and offers 42 cabins. It's a great place to stop for ice cream after your hike.

To avoid the crowds and fully enjoy your hike, arrive early. We recommend parking by 9 am at the latest (even earlier on weekends) to hike Johnston Canyon without being stuck behind a long line of people.

From the parking lot, cross a bridge to a broad path next to Johnston Canyon Lodge and Bungalows. The hike initially goes through the forest with Johnston Creek beside you. Soon, you'll need to use catwalks fixed to limestone cliffs to hike through the canyon because there is no space for a regular trail.

This trail is a 5.3 km round trip and takes an average of 2 hours to complete. It's moderately challenging and is a popular area for birdwatching, hiking, and snowshoeing. The trail is open year-round, and dogs are welcome but must be on a leash.

But how can one find the trailhead? To start the Johnston Canyon hike from Banff, take the Trans-Canada Highway towards Lake Louise. Use two ways to get to the starting point: Take the Bow Valley Parkway exit (#1A) for a scenic route and drive 18.1 km all the way to Johnston's Canyon. Alternatively, take the Trans-Canada all the way to Castle Mountain Junction, then drive back 5.5 km to reach the starting point.

The Canyon itself was named after a gold prospector and later developed by Walter Camp and his family. Although the National Park authorities now manage the canyon. Over thousands of years, the river has carved intricate and stunning shapes from the soft limestone rock. The canyon can be visited year-round and is popular in the summer when the canyon is covered in moss and greenery, and the pools are a deep blue-turquoise color. In winter, the Upper Falls freeze, creating an epic wall of ice, and it's a great time to try ice walking or ice climbing.

The Upper Canyon Falls drops 40 m into a deep plunge pool, making it a truly dramatic sight. They can be accessed via a catwalk, and there is a unique location below the falls called the "hidden cave."

The trail can be frustrating on the way down because of the crowds, but some of the views are better on the descent. The hike ends back at the Johnston Canyon Parking Lot, and visitors can head into Banff for a picnic at Central Park if they start early enough. So, let's recap this information we have:

Estimated length of time: 2-3 h
Length of trail: 5.3 km (3.3 mi)
Elevation gain: 263 m
Special equipment needed: Sturdy shoes, water
Recommended season: All year
Availability of water: Yes
Availability of restrooms: Yes
Handicap Accessibility: No
Kid-friendly: Yes
Pet-friendly: Yes, must be on a leash, leashed
Other activities allowed on trail: Running, Snowshoeing

Lake Louise Lakeshore

Lake Louise is a world-renowned destination known for its stunning turquoise waters and views of the Victoria Glacier. Every year, hundreds of thousands of visitors from all over the globe flock to this glacial lake to take in its beauty.

For those looking to enjoy their visit, the easygoing lakeshore trail is a great option to immerse yourself in the mountain environment without committing to a hefty day hike. Believe me, no trip to the Canadian Rockies is complete without a visit to the majestic Lake Louise. Its wild turquoise-blue waters, fed by glacier melt, are set against the stunning backdrop of Mount Victoria and a hanging glacier.

After taking in the spectacular scenery, visitors can explore the area through activities like hiking, climbing, skiing, or canoeing. A visit here is an experience that you will remember for a lifetime. To make the most of it, here's all you need to know.

This is the Lakeshore Pathway; it starts near the Chateau Lake Louise Hotel resort. At the entrance of the lake, in front of the resort, there is a large waterfront promenade with information signs that provide trail maps and directions to guide visitors in the right direction. The promenade is the starting point of the Lakeshore Pathway, which is marked with signs. Along the pathway's beginning are flower gardens, grass lawns, and sitting benches for visitors to relax. It is a popular spot and can get crowded with people.

From the promenade, the Lake Louise trail initially follows a paved pathway for a short distance but then switches to a well-maintained dirt path that mostly follows the shores of the lake. Trees shade some parts of the path, and while there are some exposed tree roots, it is generally an easy and scenic walk. Looking down the lake, visitors can enjoy great views of the chateau and the turquoise-colored lake, which is often dotted with canoes.

When you start the 4.5 km trail, you'll see canoe docks to your left but go right instead. It's an easy trail that takes about 1 hour and 10 minutes to complete. Lots of people go birdwatching, snowshoeing, and running here. You can go any time of the year. You'll walk by the Fairmont Chateau Lake Louise and its gardens. There you can see the Victoria Glacier up close. Start by looking at the beautiful lake and the mountain and glacier in the distance. You can try to name the other mountains before looking at the sign that tells you their names.

The trail is wide and flat, so you can push a stroller, use a wheelchair, or walk easily. You don't need to bring a lot of stuff because there aren't many hills. The water in the lake looks milky because of the rock silt from the glacier. When you reach the trail signs, you'll see a map of other trails in the area and a short hill to climb. Watch for rock climbers because this is a famous spot for climbing.

When you keep going, you'll see the glacial runoff and get a good view of the Fairmont Hotel on the other side of the lake. Keep walking until you reach a wooden bridge; that will be your turnaround point. Some people keep going on other trails, but you don't have to.

To get to the trailhead, take the exit to Lake Louise Village from the Trans-Canada Highway. If you're driving west, turn left and go straight through two sets of four-way stops. Keep going up the hill on Lake Louise Drive and turn left into the parking lot when you reach the Fairmont Chateau Lake Louise. The trail starts here.

For many adventurers, the Lakeshore Pathway is a starting point to access longer, more challenging hiking and backpacking trails that explore Lake Louise's wilderness areas, including glaciers, rockslides, alpine passes, snow-capped peaks, and alpine teahouses. In conclusion, the trial statistics look like this:

Estimated length of time: 2 hours
Length of trail: 4.5 km (2.8 mi)
Elevation gain: 108 m
Special equipment needed: Sturdy shoes, water
Recommended season: Spring, summer, autumn
Availability of water: Yes
Availability of restrooms: Yes
Handicap Accessibility: Yes, partially
Kid-friendly: Yes
Pet-friendly: Yes, must be on a leash
Other activities allowed on trail: Running, Snowshoeing, Rock climbing,

Rockpile Trail

Moraine Lake is a recognizable landmark in Canada and the Canadian Rockies. It is a beautiful turquoise-blue alpine lake that is fed by glaciers. The stunning Ten Peaks surround it. Every year, millions of visitors gather to see this breathtaking natural wonder. It was even featured on the Canadian twenty-dollar bill.

Visiting Moraine Lake is a truly unforgettable experience. The lake's natural beauty is awe-inspiring and peaceful, making visitors feel calm and relaxed. After taking in the stunning views, visitors can enjoy various outdoor activities in Banff National Park, such as hiking, climbing, skiing, or canoeing. This lake is a sight that will stay with you forever.

When visiting this lake, don't miss the Rockpile Trail. It is a short and easy hike, taking only 10 minutes to reach the summit. You can enjoy a view of the beautiful blue lake and the Valley of the 10 Peaks from a lookout named Rockpile. This is where our hike is taking us! The trail is about 0.8 km long and is moderately challenging, with an elevation gain of 10 m.

To reach the Rockpile Trail, head to the side where the washrooms are and follow the path until you reach a small bridge. Ignore the signs pointing towards Consolation Lakes, which is a longer hike, and turn right. You'll come across steps that will take you to the top in just 5 minutes. Note that the trail is not wheelchair accessible, but the lake shore is. If you can't do the hike, you can drive your vehicle to the lake if you have a handicapped sign or "Parking Placard."

Once you reach the foot of the Rockpile Trail, you'll see a sign indicating the way up. The climb might be a little challenging for some due to the high elevation and steps, so take your time. At the top, you'll be rewarded with an incredible view that pictures cannot fully capture.

If you plan to visit Moraine Lake, it's best to book a shuttle or tour in advance. Personal vehicles are no longer permitted on Moraine Lake Road due to traffic and only Parks Canada shuttles, Roam Public Transit, and commercial buses are permitted.

Moraine Lake, with its vivid turquoise waters set against the surrounding mountains, is a stunning natural feature in the Lake Louise area. It freezes over in winter and doesn't thaw until June when the rock silt from the glacier gives it its characteristic turquoise color. The view from Rockpile is so picturesque that it's featured on Canadian $20 bills from 1969 to 1979.

The area around Moraine Lake is popular for outdoor activities, such as hiking, backpacking, and cross-country skiing in the winter. You can rent canoes to cross the lake, but swimming is prohibited. The larch forests around the lake turn yellow, gold, and red in the fall. The Valley of the Ten Peaks, where Moraine Lake is located, is named after the ten stunning peaks that surround the lake. The highest peak is Deltaform Mountain, at 3,424 m, closely followed by Mount Fay. The valley is covered by forest and is ideal for hiking, backpacking, biking, and wildlife watching.

The Rockpile Trail hike is easy and suitable for families and inexperienced hikers. To start, hike through the parking lot and take the trail that goes behind the Rockpile. The trail is well-made, with steps for steeper ascents. Once at the top of the Rockpile, you can enjoy the stunning scenery of the Ten Peaks and Moraine Lake Valley. The hike continues in a circuit on top of the Rockpile, with many viewpoints for great photos. After that, head towards Moraine Lake Lodge, and hike around the lake as far as you want.

The Rockpile Trail has an iconic view of the Canadian Rockies, and experienced hikers should add it to their itinerary. Here is what to have in mind:

Estimated length of time: 1 hour
Length of trail: 0.8 km (0.5 mi)
Elevation gain: 10 m
Special equipment needed: Sturdy shoes, water
Recommended season: All year

Availability of water: Yes
Availability of restrooms: Yes
Handicap Accessibility: Yes, partially
Kid-friendly: Yes
Pet-friendly: Yes, must be on a leash
Other activities allowed on the trail: Running, Biking, Bird watching, and Picnicking. Cross-country skiing

Fenland Trail

Escape the noise of downtown Banff and experience the peaceful oasis of the Fenland Trail. This interpretive trail is just a short distance from the city center but feels like a different world. The 2 km loop takes you along creekside paths and over charming wooden bridges, surrounded by towering spruce trees and singing birds. You can truly feel the essence of Banff National Park here!

The Fenland Trail is a flat and easy walk exploring Banff's marshlands. It has many signs that teach visitors about the area and its wildlife. Families enjoy this hike, and to get there, take the Mount Norquay Road exit from the Trans-Canada Highway and turn right into the parking lot with a trail sign.

Follow the flat trail into the forest from the parking lot and cross a large wooden bridge to reach a junction. Follow the signs for Fenland Loop, staying left. Be sure to follow the trail signage, as this loop has many entry and exit points. At the next junction, turn right and follow Echo Creek as the trail narrows. Take breaks at the various benches and viewpoints along the way.

Continue along the Creekside trail, enjoying the views and listening to the highway noise when you come to a small junction with a bridge. Keep going on the trail here, as this bridge joins Vermillion Lake Road. The trail loops back to the original bridge, which you cross to return to the parking lot.

The parking lot has pit toilets and picnic tables, and you can follow the sidewalk into town along the Bow River Trail. The trail follows the banks of 40 Mile Creek and offers beautiful views of wetland marshes and wildlife, such as birds, elk, and deer. Trees surround the trail, and there are plenty of viewpoints and benches to rest and take in the scenery. The trail is easy to navigate, with interpretive brochures available at the trailhead. There are also picnic tables and grassy areas near the parking lot and trailhead.

The hike is peaceful, but the sound of the swishing branches can be a little scary. It's best to hike with a group and bring water to stay hydrated. The wetland marshes in the area provide a natural habitat for various plants and wildlife, including sedges, moss, cat tails, aspen, white spruce, poplar, and more. The creek connects to Vermillion Lakes and the Bow River, which creates a network of waterways perfect for paddling.

Estimated length of time: 1 hour
Length of trail: 2 km (1.2 mi)
Elevation gain: 56 m
Special equipment needed: Sturdy shoes, water
Recommended season: All year
Availability of water: Yes
Availability of restrooms: Yes
Handicap Accessibility: Yes

Kid-friendly: Yes
Pet-friendly: Yes, must be on a leash
Other activities allowed on trail: Running, Biking, Snowshoeing

Conclusion

As you might have seen from this chapter, Banff National Park offers numerous hikes perfect for beginners. They suit families, nature enthusiasts, and anyone else looking for a gentle or short hike. Remember that the park's trails are often well maintained and marked but also offer amazing views of the surrounding mountains.

In the end, I hope you enjoyed exploring these top four beginner hikes in Banff National Park, and now we are bound to step our game up and see the more intermediate hikes here, so stay tuned!

PUSHING YOUR LIMITS

What do you get when you combine amazing alpine views, glacial lakes, and slightly more challenging trails? Of course, you will get the best intermediate hikes in Banff National Park!

As you might have seen from our previous chapter, this National Park has numerous hiking options, even for those seeking a moderate challenge. There are numerous intermediate hikes that we will cover right now. In fact, these hikes are perfect for those comfortable with elevation gain and can handle some Rocky terrain but also know what to bring on their hikes and what to expect.

The numerous benefits of these hikes are not just health-wise but also because they offer stunning panoramic views, unique landscapes, and numerous opportunities to encounter wildlife and wild plants. All you need is a bit more effort and preparation for these intermediate hikes, but they offer much more reward.

Finally, we will now discuss the five intermediate hikes in Banff National Park. Stay tuned, and let's tackle the question of which hikes are perfect for beginner and intermediate hikers and how to conquer them.

Lake Agnes

This hike is a popular hike in Banff National Park that starts at Lake Louise. It ends at the Lake Agnes Tea House. The tea house has a long history and was named after Canada's first First Lady, Lady Agnes MacDonald.

Now, this is a fun trip to a pretty lake with a cute little tea house. Once you're at the tea house, you can choose to hike up to the Little Beehive, walk around Lake Agnes, or relax and enjoy the beautiful views while drinking tea. You can try this 7.4 km round-trip trail near Lake Louise, Alberta.

It's a bit challenging but not too hard, and it usually takes about 3 hours to finish. Many people come here to go birdwatching, hiking, or running, so you might see other people around. The best time to go is between June and October.

To avoid parking issues, arriving early at the main parking lot near Lake Louise is best. Then, follow the path around the lake, passing by the Chateau Lake Louise, until you see a sign pointing towards Lake Agnes. The uphill path will take you through the forest, offering glimpses of Lake Louise along the way. After about 2.7 km, you will reach Mirror Lake, followed by Lake Agnes about 1 km later. The Lake Agnes Tea House is a popular stop, but you might have it to yourself if you arrive early.

The tea and baked goods are delicious and will provide energy for further hiking. You can also consider two short hikes: one around Lake Agnes to the Big Beehive and the other up to the Little Beehive. To return, follow the signed route back to Lake Louise.

Along the way, hikers can see stunning natural landscapes, including Mirror Lake and Lake Agnes, as well as Mount Victoria topped by an expansive glacier. Hikers can choose to take the trail to Lake Agnes and Mirror Lake, which offers better sights along the route.

To start your hike to Lake Agnes, go to Chateau Lake Louise, which is a 10-minute drive from the village of Lake Louise and the Lake Louise Inn. From the public parking lot, walk along the paved promenade next to Lake Louise, with the Chateau on your right and the lake on your left. Look out for the Lake Agnes trail, which branches off just as the Chateau grounds end. You should see a sign that says, "Lake Agnes 3.6 km."

Don't take the main paved trail that goes all the way around the lake, as it leads to a different tea house called Plain of Six Glaciers. The Lake Agnes trail will enter the forest and cross a horse trail. Keep following the forest trail, which will get steeper at the beginning. When you reach a switchback in the trail, you'll have a clear view of Lake Louise below. Keep going uphill until you come to a horse gate and a new trail junction. Turn left/uphill after the gate, and soon you'll reach Mirror Lake. From there, you can see the Tea House. It is to the right of the "Big Beehive." To get to the Tea House, take the trail to the right from Mirror Lake and follow it straight. The stairs are the last part of the hike.

After hiking to Lake Agnes Tea House, you can take two short hikes. One option is to walk around the far end of Lake Agnes, which is only 800 m away. You can see a better view of the valley and the tea house from there. However, this route is dangerous during winter when there is still snow in the mountains. Another option is to hike up to the Little Beehive, an 850 m hike with a 100 m elevation gain. To return, head back to the tea house and follow your route, passing Mirror Lake and then Lake Louise.

Remember to start early in the morning or late in the afternoon. This is to avoid crowds and parking issues. If the tea house is crowded, go to the end of the lake for a quieter spot, and there are ways to extend your hike, such as going up to Mt. St. Piran or over to Plain of the 6 Glaciers via Big Beehive.

But how can one get there? To get to the trailhead, drive towards Chateau Lake Louise and park on the left side. However, parking is limited and often full by 8 am. Alternatively, you can take a shuttle. Use the Lake Louise Overflow Parking Lot provided by Parks Canada. Here are the stats for this hike:

Estimated length of time: 3 hours
Length of trail: 7.4 km (4.5 mi)
Elevation gain: 435 m
Special equipment needed: Sturdy shoes, water, trekking poles, nutrition, rain gear, first aid
Recommended season: Summer - Autumn
Availability of water: Yes
Availability of restrooms: Yes
Handicap Accessibility: No
Kid-friendly: Yes
Pet-friendly: Yes, must be on a leash
Other activities allowed on trail: Running, Biking, Snowshoeing, Cross-country skiing

Tunnel Mountain Summit

Escape the busy streets of Banff with a quick hike up Tunnel Mountain. From the top, you'll enjoy stunning views that make you feel like you're surrounded by wilderness, even though Banff Avenue is only a kilometer away.

Discover the 4.3 km Tunnel Mountain trail near Banff, Alberta. Although it's considered moderately challenging, most people complete it in under 2 hours. The area is popular for hiking, snowshoeing, and running, so you'll likely see other outdoor enthusiasts. The trail is open year-round and is equally beautiful in all seasons.

Turn right along St. Julien Road when you get to the "T" and walk until you see a grass-covered lawn on your left. The path to Tunnel Mountain is well-marked and goes up from the left-hand side of the parking lot. After crossing another road, the hike consists of moderate switchbacks that offer glimpses of Banff town and the mountains. You'll hear the sounds of animals and birds instead of road noise.

The hike starts on the mountain's eastern slope, where a forest will surround you. As you hike up the switchbacks, you'll have plenty of opportunities to stop. Then, you can enjoy the breathtaking views of the Banff Springs Hotel and the mountains surrounding the Bow Valley.

As you approach the summit, the trail will turn north and follow a ridgeline, allowing you to enjoy views in both directions. There are safety rails along the mountain's west side to protect hikers from a fatal drop, but they also provide a fantastic vantage point for admiring the views to the west, including the Bow River valley.

Near the top, you'll reach a viewpoint where Parks Canada has placed two iconic red chairs, perfect for snapping a photo for your social media feed. It is one of the best viewpoints in Banff, making the Tunnel Mountain hike a popular and Instagram-worthy destination year-round.

At the final switchback, you'll see a ledge with railings. Be careful and keep children close by. When you reach the top, you will be rewarded with a beautiful viewing area where you can relax and have a snack. You can also explore a grassy meadow that is just a short walk away.

To go down from Tunnel Mountain, follow the same route you came up on. Start your hike early or late in the day to avoid the crowds. It is a popular trail, so it's busy. You can access the Tunnel Mountain Trailhead on foot from Banff Avenue or park on St. Julien Road if you're driving.

Despite its name, it's actually a big hill at 1,684 m above sea level. But don't let that stop you from enjoying the panoramic views of the Banff Townsite, Banff Springs Hotel, Bow Valley, and surrounding mountains.

Tunnel Mountain in Banff is a beautiful place for outdoor activities. There are trails for different levels of experience, and the views of the other mountains and Bow Valley are stunning. Wild animals like elk, bighorn sheep, and mountain goats can also be seen.

The mountain is named after a tunnel that was once planned but never built for the Canadian Pacific Railway. It is a great place to enjoy the natural beauty of the Canadian Rockies, whether you want peace and quiet or an exciting adventure. Here is what you need to know about this hike:

Estimated length of time: 3 hours
Length of trail: 4.3 km (2.7 mi)
Elevation gain: 268 m
Special equipment needed: Sturdy shoes, water, trekking poles, nutrition, rain gear, first aid
Recommended season: All year
Availability of water: Yes
Availability of restrooms: Yes
Handicap Accessibility: No
Kid-friendly: Yes
Pet-friendly: Yes, must be on a leash
Other activities allowed on trail: Running, Biking, Snowshoeing, Cross-country skiing

Sulphur Mountain Trail

Locals love the Sulphur Mountain hike, but it is often missed by tourists who are distracted by the Banff Gondola. The gondola takes people to a fancy building with restaurants and fabulous views, but it costs money. If you enjoy a hike, try the Sulphur Mountain Trail instead. Although it's not the most scenic mountain in Banff, it's still a popular place to hike and take in the fresh air.

The trail is 10.8 km long and takes about 4.5 hours to complete. Many people come here to hike, snowshoe, or run, so you'll likely see other people on the trail. It's open all year, and dogs are welcome, but they need to be on a leash.

To see the majestic Cascade Mountain and Sundance Range peaks, you can take the Sulphur Mountain hike or ride the Banff Gondola, which has restaurants, hiking trails, and observation decks at the summit. The gondola is wheelchair accessible, making it possible for those with limited mobility to reach the top. In summer, Sulphur Mountain can be crowded due to its easy accessibility.

Sulphur Mountain is named after the two sulfurous hot springs found on its lower slopes. The hot springs were initially set aside as a nature preserve by Prime Minister John A. Macdonald after a dispute over their ownership. Later, the act expanded the park and included Sulphur Mountain.

The park continued to grow in popularity among tourists, particularly the wealthy, who were drawn to the area for its serenity and mountain sports. It wasn't until 1930 and the passing of the National Park Act that Banff National Park was significantly expanded and given its current name.

To reach the Sulphur Mountain trailhead, start in the town of Banff, go south on Banff Avenue toward the Bow River, cross the bridge, and turn left, staying in the right lane. Yield right onto Mountain Ave immediately after turning left. Continue for 4.5 km on the winding road and take the first right off the traffic circle to the Banff Upper Hot Springs parking lot. You'll see a trail sign on the right-hand side.

The town of Banff's original weather station was located on Sulphur Mountain. The observatory was constructed in 1903 and is now the upper gondola station. In 1956, the Sulphur Mountain Cosmic Ray Station was established 1.1 km from the main observatory, a National Historic Site. Hikers can walk the 1.1 km boardwalk to see the station.

To begin the Sulphur Mountain hike, go to the Upper Hot Springs parking lot located beneath the pools on the left side. Start climbing up the slope and curve right to start the switchbacks. There are 28 switchbacks in total, but they make the climb's incline easier. Don't count them on your way up, as it won't make the trail go by faster.

While ascending the local trail, appreciate the forest as you walk underneath the gondola line. Passengers on the gondola will likely cheer and encourage you to make it to the top. Keep following the switchbacks until you reach a cobblestone pad near the upper gondola station. Follow the signs around the building to explore the facilities or to extend your hike to the Cosmic Ray Station.

At the summit, you'll enjoy breathtaking panoramic views, including one of the best views of the town. This trail's numerous switchbacks make the hike very rewarding. After finishing the hike, unwind by visiting the Banff Upper Hot Springs below.

One can also take the gondola up the mountain. The Banff Sightseeing Gondola, just five minutes from the Town of Banff, is one of the most popular activities in Banff throughout the year. It offers breathtaking views of the six mountain ranges from the top of Sulphur Mountain without the effort of hiking up and down.

The Banff Gondola provides an opportunity to unwind and enjoy the scenery year-round. Although the gondola is quite pricey at $62 CAD ($46 USD) for a round trip, it's an excellent alternative for people who are unable to complete the Sulphur Mountain hike, such as individuals with disabilities, seniors, or large families with young children. One-way tickets are also available if you don't want to take the hike back down or if you just want to experience the gondola.

However, if you are physically capable, I strongly recommend hiking up Sulphur Mountain rather than spending money on the Banff Gondola. The stunning views will be even more satisfying after burning some calories on the hike. These are the tips I have for you concerning this hike:

Estimated length of time: 4 hours
Length of trail: 10 km (6.2 mi)
Elevation gain: 759 m
Special equipment needed: Sturdy shoes, water, trekking poles, nutrition, rain gear, first aid
Recommended season: All year
Availability of water: Yes
Availability of restrooms: Yes
Handicap Accessibility: No
Kid-friendly: Yes
Pet-friendly: Yes, must be on a leash
Other activities allowed on trail: Running, Snowshoeing, Cross-country skiing

Johnston Canyon to Ink Pots

Discover this 11.3 km out-and-back trail, it is considered moderately challenging. The area is well-known for birding, hiking, and snowshoeing, and it's common to run into other explorers while on the trail. That even goes for winter when I recommend trying this hike out.

The trail is accessible year-round and offers stunning views regardless of the season. The snowshoe trail is a must-try experience, taking hikers through the breathtaking frozen landscape of Johnston Canyon before leading into a peaceful forest. The trail eventually opens up to a subalpine meadow where visitors can find a frozen lake.

The Ink Pots basin is an awe-inspiring sight featuring strikingly colored blue and green pools of water. It's a hike that's definitely worth the effort and worth doing there and back. These cold-water springs are named after ink wells and are colored by minerals that give them their vivid shades, maintaining a temperature of 4 degrees Celsius throughout the year.

To begin the hike, start at the Johnston Canyon Resort and follow the trail up to the falls, which will alternate between dirt paths and elevated walkways. These paths can get crowded in the summer, so patience may be required to navigate through people with photography gear.

After a leisurely 2.7-kilometer uphill trek, you'll arrive at the falls. Take a break to admire the breathtaking view and be sure to visit both the upper and lower viewing platforms to appreciate the beauty of the falls.

From there, continue on the path, keeping right at the junction for the Ink Pots, and follow the well-maintained trail as it narrows. The route begins to descend after a 5.3 km hike, and you'll emerge from the forest. Continue following the trail to reach the basin where the Ink Pots are situated, with frequently walked paths weaving among them. Even if the Ink Pots are not as impressive as you had hoped, the views of Johnston Creek will surely lift your spirits.

During winter, Johnston Canyon can be hazardous as it becomes an entirely ice-covered wonderland. Wearing snowshoes is recommended; some may opt for spikes or crampons to use on the catwalk sections before switching to snowshoes. However, snowshoes should provide enough traction if the conditions are not too icy. The first section of the trail through the canyon can be quite crowded due to tour groups and guided trips, but after the upper falls, you can enjoy a quiet forest before reaching the Ink Pots.

If you want to extend your Johnston Canyon trip, snowshoeing to the Ink Pots is an excellent way to do so. It will double your distance and offer a view of what lies beyond the canyon. After you've explored the waterfall, return to the junction, and take the left trail to the waterfall overlook, where you can stand atop the falls and enjoy the view. Then, return to the junction and start your journey to the Ink Pots.

The trail will ascend through the forest for 2 km before descending to the meadows. Be cautious when descending, as it can be steep in some sections. Once you reach the meadows, continue along the trail for 500 m until you reach the Ink Pots. You'll find benches and trails that circumnavigate the small frozen pools here.

Take your time and appreciate the peacefulness of the subalpine meadows before heading back the same way you came. It's a good idea to bring microspikes or crampons in case the conditions are icier than usual. To reach Johnston Canyon, drive westbound on the Trans-Canada Highway from the Town of Banff for 32 km until you reach Castle Junction. Cross the bridge and turn right onto the Bow Valley Parkway. After driving for 6 km, you'll see the Johnston Canyon parking lot on your left.

Estimated length of time: 4 hours
Length of trail: 11.3 km (7 mi)
Elevation gain: 567 m
Special equipment needed: Sturdy shoes, microspikes or crampons, snowshoes, water, trekking poles, nutrition, first aid
Recommended season: Winter
Availability of water: Yes
Availability of restrooms: Yes
Handicap Accessibility: No
Kid-friendly: Yes
Pet-friendly: Yes, must be on a leash
Other activities allowed on trail: Snowshoeing, Cross-country skiing

Plain of Six Glaciers Trail

It is a well-known trail in Banff National Park, taking you past Lake Louise, up to a charming Tea House, and concluding with breathtaking views of glaciers. It also provides an exclusive alternative route that goes through The Highline Trail, leading up to Big Beehive and descending to Lake Agnes.

This out-and-back trail, near Lake Louise, Alberta, spans 14.6 km and is generally considered moderately challenging. The area is popular for hiking, birdwatching, and horseback riding, so expect to come across other people while exploring. The trail is open year-round and is stunning no matter when you visit.

If you want to see glaciers and witness their incredible power, you can go here. It's a popular hiking spot where you can hear the sound of ice scraping against a rock as you make your way up the trail. The Plain is named after several glaciers, including Lefroy, Mount Aberdeen, Victoria, Lower Victoria, and Pope's Peak. You can see some of these glaciers from the tea house, too.

As you keep hiking up, you'll also see the historic Abbot Pass hut the Swiss guides built in 1922 for mountaineers. It's named after Philip Stanley Abbot, who died while trying to climb Mount Lefroy in 1896.

The local Tea House is a popular spot for hikers to rest and enjoy the stunning views of the mountains and glaciers. It was built in 1927 for the Canadian Pacific Railway and has maintained its traditional features and practices. The tea house has been owned and operated by the same family since 1959, and they either helicopter in or carry supplies up themselves. They only accept cash for payment.

The hike starts from the Lake Louise parking lot and follows the path to the right, passing by the Chateau Lake Louise, which is usually crowded with tourists taking pictures. After passing over a delta created by the glacier's silt deposits, the crowds start to subside, and hikers anticipate reaching the Plain of Six Glaciers viewpoint.

The trail climbs up, thinning the forest and granting views down to Lake Louise and the valley below. After 5.5 km of hiking, hikers reach the Plain of the Six Glaciers Tea House. The Abbots Pass Viewpoint, about 1.5 km farther along, is also an excellent spot to stop and enjoy the incredible views.

Hikers can retrace their steps to return to Lake Louise or take an alternate route, the Highline Trail, up to the Big Beehive and down to Lake Agnes. This alternate route is more challenging, with a total distance of 19.4 km and an elevation gain of 905 m. Hikers can take the alternate route back to Lake Louise by hiking back to the Tea House, then continuing on the path for 1.5 km towards Lake Louise until they reach the trailhead.

Arriving at Lake Louise early to secure a parking spot or take a bus or taxi, especially during peak season, is advisable. A parking spot at the Lake Louise parking lot can be secured if one arrives before 8 am, but if that is not possible, a bus or taxi from Lake Louise can take you there.

Estimated length of time: 5 hours
Length of trail: 14.6 km (9 mi)
Elevation gain: 588 m
Special equipment needed: Sturdy shoes, water, trekking poles, rain gear, nutrition, first aid
Recommended season: Summer and Autumn
Availability of water: Yes
Availability of restrooms: Yes
Handicap Accessibility: No
Kid-friendly: Yes
Pet-friendly: Yes, must be on a leashPet-friendly: Yes, must be on a leashash

Other activities allowed on trail: Snowshoeing, Cross-country skiing, Running, Horseback riding, Bird watching

Conclusion

I hope you enjoyed our discussion about the intermediate hikes in Banff National Park. Indeed, Lake Agnes, Tunnel Mountain, and Plain of Six Glaciers are excellent trails that I recommend you try.

Next, we will talk about the most challenging hikes in this National Park, which you can take to the next level. Still, you will need to be cautious because your safety and the safety of your group is in your hands. Nevertheless, make sure you enjoy your hike and be prepared for the next chapter.

SCALING NEW HEIGHTS

Finally, we reached the section of the advanced hike. These hikes are typically those that involve challenging terrain, steep climbs, and longer distances. Needless to say, as their name says, they are for advanced hikers that know what they're doing. They require a higher level of physical fitness and a certain hiking experience.

They are longer and steeper than moderate and beginner hikes. If you're ready to take your hiking to the next level and have already managed some intermediate hikes, or if you're already a seasoned hiker, these advanced hikes will test your limits. If you aim to push yourself to new heights and scale them, these hikes are perfect for you.

In this chapter, we will finally delve into the three most challenging hikes in Banff National Park, which include the Big Beehive, Sentinel Pass, and Devil's Thumb, so stay tuned.

Big Beehive

The Big Beehive hike is a favorite in Banff National Park because it includes visiting a historic tea house and climbing to a breathtaking viewpoint overlooking Lake Louise. The trail has a mix of scenery and experiences. At first, it is a moderate uphill hike in the forest, a scenic walk by the lakeshore, and ending with a challenging climb to the top of Big Beehive.

The hike also offers some flexibility in terms of route, as it can be done as an out and back or a loop. This 10.8 km trail is generally considered challenging, but starting at Lake Louise is satisfying and gets better as you continue. It's a popular area for birding, hiking, and snowshoeing, so expect to encounter other people while exploring. The best times to visit are from June through October.

The Big Beehive hike can get very crowded during the summer in Lake Louise. The trailhead is located on the busy Lake Louise Lakeshore and continues on towards the Lake Agnes trail. However, the crowds will thin out as you continue on the trail and move away from the trailhead. It's important to leave early to avoid the crowds and get a good view of Lake Louise from the Big Beehive lookout.

The hike gets its name from the reflection it casts on Mirror Lake. As you hike, you will pass several small alpine lakes and a historic teahouse and eventually reach the Big Beehive viewpoint, where you can admire the turquoise waters of Lake Louise from above.

Although Lake Louise is a popular destination on its own, the view from the Big Beehive lookout offers a unique perspective. To get to the Big Beehive, follow the lakeshore to the right and look for signs of Lake Agnes. Despite the crowds, make sure to take in the views of Lake Louise as you gain elevation.

Some hikers end their journey at Mirror Lake and view the Big Beehive towering above. Climb the stairs at the small waterfall to the historic Lake Agnes teahouse and enjoy a break on the deck. The trail will then lead you around the back of the lake to switchbacks that take you to the Big Beehive viewpoint.

At the junction atop the switchbacks, you can choose to either go back the way you came or take the Highline Trail to the Plain of Six Glaciers trail, where you can extend your hike and visit the historic tea house with views of the Victoria Glacier and Abbott Pass. All trails are well-marked, so finding your way shouldn't be a problem.

To start the Big Beehive hike, you must go to Lake Louise. If you're coming from Banff, take the Trans-Canada Highway heading west for 57.0 km and exit at Lake Louise. After the ramp, go straight through two sets of four-way stops and continue uphill on Lake Louise Drive, passing other lodges and hotels until you reach Fairmont Chateau Lake Louise. Turn left into the public parking lot when you arrive at the Chateau, follow signs to the lake, and turn right along the lakeshore. From there, you'll see signs for the Big Beehive trail.

The Big Beehive Trail is an excellent choice for those who want to enjoy beautiful alpine views without having to tackle a very challenging hike. Although there are some tricky parts, the overall difficulty level of the Big Beehive hike is moderate and manageable for most hikers.

Estimated length of time: 3 hours
Length of trail: 10.8 km (6.7 mi)
Elevation gain: 778 m

Special equipment needed: Sturdy shoes, water, trekking poles, rain gear, nutrition, first aid
Recommended season: All year, best in summer
Availability of water: Yes
Availability of restrooms: Yes
Handicap Accessibility: No
Kid-friendly: Yes
Pet-friendly: Yes, must be on a leash
Other activities allowed on trail: Snowshoeing, Cross-country skiing, Running, Horseback riding, Bird watching

Sentinel Pass

This trail is 11.1 kilometers long and is considered a challenging route. Many people enjoy birdwatching, hiking, and running in this area, so you'll likely see others while you explore. The best time to visit this trail is from June to October. The Sentinel Pass hike is a great way to see some of Canada's most incredible natural wonders in Lake Louise. The hike begins at Moraine Lake and takes you through beautiful native larches to an alpine pass with incredible views - an unforgettable experience.

The Sentinel Pass is the highest point on this trail and offers a breathtaking view of the Valley of the Ten Peaks and surrounding mountains in Banff National Park. From the pass, you can see Paradise Valley, Mount Lefroy, Mount Aberdeen, and Haddo Peak. You can also catch a glimpse of Collier Peak and Pope's Peak to the east and the Ten Peaks to the south.

The Grand Sentinel, a large rock spire on the northern side of Pinnacle Mountain, gave the pass its name. This towering quartzite rock obelisk stands over 100 m high and is a popular challenge for rock climbers. The Valley of the Ten Peaks is named after the ten imposing peaks that crown the valley. Although there are more than ten mountains surrounding the valley, the name was derived from the ten peaks identified by Samuel Allen, an explorer of the region, who named the surrounding mountains according to the numbers 1-10 in the language of the Stoney First Nations.

To hike the Sentinel Pass, you may need to join a group of 4-6 people during certain times of the year. To avoid crowds, arrive early or start after 4 pm and bring a picnic to enjoy dinner in the meadow below the pass. If you're lucky and the weather is calm, you might get to see a beautiful reflection of the Ten Peaks on one of the lakes.

To get to the Sentinel Pass trailhead consider booking a shuttle or tour due to the 2023 road closure on Moraine Lake Road.

To start the Sentinel Pass Trail, walk towards the lake, keeping the lake on your left-hand side. Follow the trail markers until you see the sign indicating the start of the Sentinel Pass Trail on the right-hand side. Note that this area is a prime bear habitat, so it's important to hike in groups to limit bear encounters. If you don't have a large enough group, hike together with another group to meet the minimum size requirements.

The Sentinel Pass Trail starts with a steep climb through the forest, with rocks and tree roots along the way. It's not recommended to bring strollers or wheelchairs due to the rugged terrain. Along the way, you'll catch glimpses of the turquoise waters of Lake Moraine and the Ten Peaks through the trees. After a while, you'll reach a junction where you can turn off for Eiffel Lake but continue straight to Sentinel Pass. You'll notice the trail leveling off and larch trees becoming predominant. Take a quick break at the small stream with a log bridge before continuing on to the tiring but rewarding journey ahead.

As you emerge from the trees, you'll be in an exquisite meadow with three beautiful lakes. The largest of these, the first you encounter, can still have ice well into summer. The pass will be straight ahead as you approach the tree line. Look ahead and to the right for a path cut across a mountain with switchbacks up to the pass. Be prepared for steep climbing and potential snow patches. Hikers without hiking boots or poles may turn back, though there are "boot packs" through the snow.

Enjoy a view down into Paradise Valley at the pass but be cautious of the dangerous drops off the small rock outcroppings on either side. You may also see experienced scramblers taking the path toward Mount Temple, but this route is only for those with helmets and scrambling experience.

The highlight of the hike is coming down from Sentinel Pass with an expanding view of the Valley of Ten Peaks. Take a break in the alpine meadow before the pleasant descent back to Moraine Lake. The uphill trek will be much easier going down, and soon you'll be back at the beautiful Moraine Lake.

Estimated length of time: 5 hours
Length of trail: 11.1 km (6.9 mi)
Elevation gain: 799 m

Special equipment needed: Sturdy shoes, water, trekking poles, rain gear, nutrition, first aid
Recommended season: All year
Availability of water: Yes
Availability of restrooms: Yes
Handicap Accessibility: No
Kid-friendly: Yes
Pet-friendly: Yes, must be on a leash
Other activities allowed on trail: Snowshoeing, Biking, Cross-country skiing, Running, Horseback riding, Bird watching

Devil's Thumb

Devil's Thumb is a 12.7 km round-trip trail, considered challenging, but many people enjoy hiking and running here. The best time to visit is between June and October, and you can bring your dog as long as it's on a leash. As you scramble up Devil's Thumb, you'll see famous landmarks on the way. When you get to the Big Beehive junction, you'll leave the crowds behind and take the less-traveled route for stunning views of Lake Louise and Lake Agnes from high above. If the conditions are right, you might see the Devil's Thumb casting a thumb-shaped shadow below. It's a great spot to enjoy solitude and stunning views.

If you want to hike the Devil's Thumb trail from the lakeshore of Lake Louise, keep in mind that there are no signs for the trail. Instead, follow the signs for the Big Beehive and then embark on the true Devil's Thumb route.

It is a scramble route, so make sure to pay attention. Watch out for the route description before you head out. Although it requires a bit more route-finding than an average hike, it is not too difficult for a scramble. You don't need a helmet, but make sure to wear sturdy shoes as there are slippery sections with loose rock.

This trail takes you through many of the famous Lake Louise landmarks before reaching new heights away from the crowds. The Devil's Thumb is not a well-known route and requires a bit more skill to reach the top, so that you won't see many people on it. The Devil's Thumb is a good option if you want something more adventurous in the Lake Louise area.

To get to the Devil's Thumb trailhead, follow the well-beaten path up to Lake Agnes. You will find that the first portion of the trail is effortless, but it is a popular route leading to many destinations accessible to beginner hikers.

As you climb up the trail to Mirror Lake and Lake Agnes, enjoy the views of the lake. The historic teahouse at Lake Agnes is a perfect spot for a break. Follow the trail around the mountain and take the right junction towards the Devil's Thumb. The unmarked trail may seem a bit odd but continue forward. You are on the right path. You will reach a small rock band that is easy to navigate and then follow the winding path around the mountain to see incredible views of the surrounding peaks.

After about twenty minutes, you will reach a very steep, rocky, and grassy slope. Ascend this slope, and then head right towards the Devil's Thumb when you reach the saddle at the top. Work your way through the rocks until you find yourself at the edge of the Devil's Thumb. Enjoy the incredible views of the lakes.

To descend, retrace your steps and return the way you came. Insider hints for the Devil's Thumb include going early to avoid crowds, knowing the route description before leaving the main trail, bringing poles for the scramble descent, and taking a break at the famous historic teahouse on your way up or down. To get to the Devil's Thumb trailhead, start from Lake Louise and follow the signs to the right. Although there is no sign for the Devil's Thumb, follow the signs to the Big Beehive to get there.

Estimated length of time: 4 hours
Length of trail: 12.7 km (7.9 mi)
Elevation gain: 939 m
Special equipment needed: Sturdy shoes, water, trekking poles, rain gear, nutrition, first aid
Recommended season: All year
Availability of water: Yes
Availability of restrooms: Yes
Handicap Accessibility: No
Kid-friendly: Yes
Pet-friendly: Yes, must be on a leash
Other activities allowed on trail: Snowshoeing, Biking, Cross-country skiing, Running, Horseback riding, Bird watching

Conclusion

If you are considering trying one of these expert hikes, make sure to bring all the needed gear and adequately prepare yourself. Also, you need to assess your abilities and not try any of these hikes if you're not feeling fit for them. I hope you have understood that these hikes might be hard but not impossible. In fact, every advanced hiker can do them, but they will test your limits.

This chapter talked about the three most challenging hikes here in Banff National Park, and now as we have finished our hiking chapters of the book, it is time to give you a few tips before running out to hike, preparing you for a trip with your children and dogs.

BRINGING THE WHOLE PACK

Every nature lover has heard the quote: "The mountains are calling, and I must go" by John Muir. We ourselves feel this calling, and while our partners and friends might hear the calling too, not all pieces of the puzzle can fit together. In fact, some members of our pack might not be ready for an adventure. Therefore, I wrote this chapter which will help you gain some knowledge, provide tips, and give you advice for hiking with your children and your dogs so the whole family can join in.

You might be worried about your little ones and furry friends, but this chapter will explore the joys and challenges of hiking. We will cover things like hiking with kids but also hiking with pets. I will provide you with some tips on making the whole process fun but also extra safe for everyone.

As I've covered before, in one of the first chapters, hiking is a wonderful way to escape the hustle and bustle. I know I use it to reconnect with nature and stay physically active. But it's not like this for everyone!

Not only is it a great solo activity, but it's also perfect for sharing with your family, including your furry friends. Therefore, I believe they should come along too. However, taking kids and pets together on a hike can require extra planning. Keep in mind the precautions and careful planning to ensure everyone has a good experience.

Therefore, it might not be for everyone, especially beginners. In this article, we'll delve into the best practices for hiking with kids and pets and share tips on how to keep everyone happy and healthy on the trail. Therefore, stay tuned to learn more about both of these groups.

Hiking With Kids

Don't let becoming a parent hold you back from hiking adventures! Even if you have children or are new to hiking, it's an excellent opportunity for family outings and vacations. You may wonder if it's worth taking your kids hiking, but the answer is a resounding yes! In today's world of digital entertainment, it's important for both age groups to get outside, move their bodies, and breathe fresh air. Hiking offers a chance to escape city pollution and has numerous proven benefits for physical and mental health. The long-term benefits of hiking with children are worth the effort.

Children today often prefer digital entertainment over playing outside, but this sedentary lifestyle can lead to insomnia, anxiety, and depression. Therefore, stepping outside, moving our bodies, and breathing fresh air away from city pollution is crucial.

Studies have shown that spending time outside and being active is beneficial for both children and adults. Taking your kids on a hike is a great way to get them outside, but it may not be easy at first. However, the long-term benefits of hiking with children are definitely worth the initial effort.

It is a great way to introduce them to nature and the outdoors for a lifetime. To be prepared, it's important for adults to bring the ten essentials, such as water, snacks, sunscreen, and appropriate clothing and footwear. Once your backpack is ready with items like trail mix, reusable water bottles, a map, and a first aid kit, it's time to make the most of this special time together!

Why Hike with Kids?

Here are a few reasons why I hike with my kids:

- **Spending quality family time:** If you want to spend quality time with your family and disconnect from technology, use this to bond with your kids and create positive memories in the great outdoors.
- **Connecting with nature:** Hiking lets children develop a lifelong relationship with nature, escape the concrete jungle, and appreciate the beauty of the outdoors. It can also inspire them to become environmental stewards.
- **Exercise:** Hiking is good exercise for both you and your children. It can improve cardio-respiratory fitness, help burn calories, and prevent medical conditions like diabetes and high blood pressure.
- **Educational opportunities:** Children discover and learn about their surroundings, the environment, and basic survival skills. They can explore the trail at their own pace while learning about the principles of 'leave no trace.'

- **Exposure to wildlife:** Hiking trails offer opportunities to encounter wildlife and learn the difference between wild and captive animals. It can inspire children to appreciate the wilderness as they grow older.

Hiking Benefits for Kids

Hiking is not just a good physical workout, but research has shown that it also provides numerous cognitive, psychological, and social benefits to children. Here are some of the benefits for kids in the outdoors:

- **It helps children to test their limits:** By trying new things and taking age-appropriate risks, children can gain self-confidence and overcome their fears. Hiking provides opportunities for children to see what they're capable of and improve their skills and accomplish new feats. Overcoming obstacles, such as a challenging trail or slope, can leave children feeling empowered.
- **It may boost cognitive abilities:** Spending time in nature learning about plants, animals, geology, and geography offers opportunities for children to think critically, use their own perceptions, apply undivided attention, and use their recollection skills. Engaging children mentally through recreational activities, such as hiking, can be great for their cognitive abilities.
- **It creates opportunities for sensory learning:** Early childhood learning often comes through the engagement of the senses. Hiking offers numerous chances for children to engage their senses and improve their skills at more complex learning tasks as we advance. It also supports both motor and language development.

- **It allows for opportunities to teach in different ways:** Hiking offers opportunities for integrated learning in math, geology, biology, and history. Learning outside the classroom can come in especially handy for parents acting as secondary educators.

- **It helps children to avoid focusing on negative thoughts:** Hiking can help break the cycle of negative thoughts and energy, refocusing children's thoughts and energy onto something more positive. In one study, 90 minutes spent in a green setting was enough to lead to a self-reported reduction in negative thoughts.

- **It may improve their mental health during adulthood**: Hiking has been correlated with improved mental health in adulthood. Spending time in nature is associated with short-term improvements in mental health, making it important for parents to prioritize engaging in self-care.

How To Go Hiking with Your Kids

I'm glad you followed up because this means you have decided to take your kids hiking. It's not that hard, I promise. I will now cover how to go hiking with your kids. To choose the right hiking gear for kids, consider their age, physical abilities, and preferences. Without the proper gear, the experience may not be enjoyable. Here are a few questions you need to have answered:

How far can children hike? Kids' ability to hike varies depending on their age, so it's important to consider their boredom and tantrums. As a general rule, kids can hike half a mile for every year of age. Carrying them is necessary for ages 0-3, while kids ages 4-7 can hike 2-4 miles. Children ages 8 and up can manage more miles, but carrying a backpack may decrease their stamina.

When can they carry their own backpack? Kids ages 4 and up can carry their own daypack, but the weight will vary by age and physical ability. An appropriately sized backpack with adjustable straps is essential. The weight of the empty backpack should also be considered. A good hike for kids is engaging, fun, and kid led.

What should they wear when hiking? Children should wear weather and trail-appropriate clothing and shoes. Lightweight long sleeves and long pants are ideal in the summertime. Planning hiking games and choosing hikes with natural features is a great bet.

What makes a good hike for children? How do you choose a route that suits the whole family? They may need to take breaks, eat snacks, and play along the way. To make hiking with kids more enjoyable, consider choosing shorter hikes with interesting features such as waterfalls or rock scrambles, and look for shaded areas and benches. Plan some fun activities for the kids, like a nature-themed scavenger hunt or I Spy, to keep them engaged and entertained.

Hiking gear checklist for kids

This guide will walk you through various items to consider when it comes to kids' hiking gear, and they include:

For Toddlers:

☐ Water bottle

- ☐ Shoes
- ☐ Poles
- ☐ Walkie talkies
- ☐ Sun hat
- ☐ Base layers
- ☐ Rain gear
- ☐ Binoculars
- ☐ Daypack

For Kids:

- ☐ Daypack
- ☐ Hiking boots or shoes, socks
- ☐ Pants
- ☐ Jackets
- ☐ Water bottles
- ☐ Sun protection
- ☐ Safety gear
- ☐ Snacks

Safety Reminders

As a parent, safety is your number one priority. That is why I prepared this list of must-know tricks for you and your kids while hiking:

Brush up on bear safety tips if you're in an area with bears and learn about snake risks if you are in an area where snakes are common.

If you're hiking in mountainous areas, be prepared for quickly changing weather.

Consider hiring a guide if you're not familiar with the area or feel unsure about your ability to handle potential hazards.

Always be prepared and know your signalization! If your children think they are lost, they should stay in one place and follow the hiking emergency protocol.

Teach them not to be afraid of getting in trouble if they are lost and to make noise by singing, whistling, or telling a story to feel better.

Using small bribes or rewards can be a helpful tactic to keep kids motivated and engaged during the hike. Promising a tasty picnic lunch or an ice cream at the end of the day can help keep spirits high.

Tips for Hiking

Hiking in the mountains can be unpredictable, so being prepared is important. Children are no exception and should follow the same hiking code as everyone else. Here is what I recommend:

Before embarking on a hike, make sure your children are familiar with the hiking essentials, such as dressing appropriately. Encourage them to wear sneakers or hiking boots instead of sandals and bring a warm jacket, even if it's warm at home. The temperature can be cooler in the woods and the mountains.

Teach your children to always carry their own gear in case they get separated from the group. They should also be responsible hikers and carry all their trash out.

Children should always hike with a buddy or group and wait at all trail junctions. Advise them never to play hide and seek on a hike.

Finally, tell your children not to be afraid of wild animals. Animals don't typically like to be near people. If they hear a noise, they should make a noise back. If it's an animal, it will likely run away. If it's a rescuer, they'll be able to find you.

Hiking With Dogs

Hiking with kids is one thing; hiking with dogs is another! If you're a hiker who also happens to be a dog owner, you and your furry friend can make great trail buddies. However, your canine companion will require a lot of care and attention, especially at first. It's important to remember that this is part of the commitment you've made, so consider the following advice to help turn your dog into the perfect trail partner.

Having a dog as a hiking companion can be incredibly rewarding, as they're always eager and ready to hit the trail. Plus, hiking with your dog can provide you and your pet with a range of health benefits while deepening your bond through shared experiences.

But why would one want to take their dog hiking? Is it that simple? Walking and hiking are excellent ways for both of you to stay fit, work on mental health, and maintain a healthy weight. Lack of exercise can lead to chronic health problems and arthritis. Regular walks and hikes reduce these risks by providing regular exercise, and studies have shown that dog owners get more exercise per day than those without dogs. Hiking adds to the workout with activities like jumping over streams and climbing rocks.

Regular walks and hikes also provide mental stimulation for dogs, as they get to experience new sights, smells, and encounters with other dogs and people. That helps to prevent boredom and destructive behavior, such as chewing and digging, which can result from a lack of stimulation.

Spending time with your dog on walks and hikes helps to strengthen the bond between you two. Sharing experiences and having a mutual give-and-take of time and energy can deepen the connection between you and your dog.

How to Take Your Dog Hiking?

Can you already see that tail wagging? Imagine your dog's happiness since you've decided to take him hiking with you. Now, I will talk about the main considerations when hiking with your dog.

- **Consult with Your Vet:** Before you and your dog go hiking, ask your veterinarian the following: Is your dog physically capable? Is your dog's immune system prepared? Are there any specific vaccinations?
- **Familiarize Yourself with Trail Regulations:** Always check the rules and regulations for the areas where you plan to hike. In most United States National Parks, even leashed dogs are not allowed on the trails. While dogs

are permitted on many state and local park trails, the rules vary, and leashes are typically mandatory.

- **Obedience Training and Trail Etiquette:** It is crucial to keep your dog under control at all times. By stepping off the trail, yield the right-of-way to hikers, horses, and bikes. You will need to keep your dog calm when other people and dogs pass by.

- **Leave No Trace:** When hiking, always pack out full poop bags. Leaving them on the trail for a later pick-up is also bad etiquette.

- **Start a Trail-Training Routine:** Ease your dog into hiking by starting with hour-long hikes and monitoring their energy levels afterward. If your dog is still highly active, increase the duration of the next hike. Work up to the amount of trail time you plan to spend on future hikes or backpacking trips. This gradual approach also helps strengthen city dogs' paws.

Hazards and Safety when Hiking with Your Dog

Your furry companion is vulnerable to many of the same hazards as you. Still, the concerning thing is that your dog won't understand many of them or be able to communicate when something is amiss. As such, you need to be prepared for the following:

- **Straining your dog:** Keep an eye on how long it takes for your dog's breathing and heart rate to return to normal during breaks. Take more breaks or shorten your hike for the day. If your dog is limping, this is another sign that you should stop for the day.

- **Wildlife:** Your leash is your best line of defense against large carnivores and prickly herbivores. Although many dogs don't show symptoms of Lyme disease, ticks are still a concern, so examine your dog thoroughly and remove any hitchhikers after the hike.

- **Wild plants:** Stopping your dog from chewing immediately is the best way to avoid poison or contaminated plants, as well as digestive problems. Be wary of nettles, poison oak, ivy, and sumac, which can cause discomfort for you and your dog.

- **Foxtails and injury:** These barbed seedpods, which can be found on various types of grasses in the spring and summer, can become lodged in fur and end up in sensitive areas. Avoid areas with foxtails and use tweezers to remove them right away.

- **Heat stroke:** Dogs can only regulate their body temperature differently than humans. They do it by panting and sweating through their paw pads. So be conservative by taking frequent breaks and drinking water and consider using a cooling collar if your dog keeps lying down in shady areas.

- **Waterborne pathogens:** Dogs are susceptible to many of the same waterborne pathogens as humans. The safest option is to treat water for both you and your dog.

- **Water safety:** If your dog can't swim, bring a dog PFD. Carry your dog over whitewater. Be cautious when allowing a swimmer to enter a lake; wet fur can cause your dog to become chilled in cool temperatures. Even if the weather is mild, you'll have a significant drying task before bedtime.

Doggy Hiking Checklist

When hiking with your furry companion, it's important to plan accordingly to ensure both you and your dog stay safe and healthy. Here are some critical tips and essentials to keep in mind when hiking with dogs:

- Doggy backpack
- Basic first aid kit
- Dog food and trail treats
- Water and water bowl
- Leash and collar, or harness
- Dog-friendly insect repellent
- ID tags
- Dog booties
- Poop bags
- Sun protection
- Dog coat
- Cooling collar

Dog Trail Etiquette

When hiking with a dog, it's important to keep in mind that it's a different experience than hiking alone. In order to ensure the safety of you, your dog, and others, it's essential to follow these tips for proper dog trail etiquette.

First, make sure the trail you plan to hike is dog-friendly by researching online or calling ahead. Some national parks, for example, do not allow dogs on their trails.

Some areas require leashes for dogs, so always bring one along. They need a collar with an ID tag containing your contact information. Include a fluorescent orange reflective vest if hiking during hunting season or after dark.

When passing other hikers, be courteous and give them the right of way. Step to the side or have your dog sit and stay calm. Stick to the marked trail and clean up after your dog's waste to leave no trace.

Remember to be friendly and polite to other trail users and follow all posted rules. By being responsible trail users, we can help preserve the dog-friendly nature of hiking trails for future adventures with our furry friends.

Conclusion

I hope you will soon know why I swear by bringing the whole pack. In fact, I believe no adventure is whole without our little ones or our four-legged friends. I hope you now know all the needed information for taking your kids and dogs hiking.

Remember, the goal is safety, and always have that in mind. Next, we will discuss why the leave-no-trace principles are vital in using our national parks.

MINIMIZING YOUR FOOTPRINT

As you might know, Banff National Park is quite famous. In fact, over four million people visit this National Park each year, and this puts an unbelievable strain on its natural resources. The wildlife is becoming more familiar to humans, the plants get trampled, and erosion is becoming a problem. Therefore, if you want to preserve this natural wonderland so our future generations know what Banff is like, it's critical to take action right now!

But how can one take action? All visitors need to follow the leave-no-trace principles. That is the only way we can protect and preserve the nature we have left in our national parks.

Therefore, this chapter is a takeaway that will discuss the importance of these principles both for campers and hikers alike.

It will help you understand and hopefully help you act to help preserve the environment and minimize our negative impact on nature. Therefore, it is time to explore these principles and learn how to implement them in our hiking and camping activities. This might be new for some but ensuring that we leave only footprints and take only memories is the only way we can preserve nature for the next generations. Let us clear all the leave no trace rules right now.

What Is Leave No Trace?

The Seven Principles of Leave No Trace offer a comprehensible set of guidelines for reducing our impact on the environment while enjoying outdoor activities. While initially designed for the wilderness, the Principles have been adapted in various settings, including local parks and backyards. They apply to nearly every recreational activity and address a specific topic with detailed information on minimizing damage.

Although the Seven Principles are widely known, they are subject to ongoing evaluation and revision. They conduct research and publish scholarly articles in independent journals to ensure that the Principles remain current and informed by the latest insights from experts in outdoor education, biologists, and land managers. Leave No Trace seeks to ensure a sustainable future for the planet and the outdoors by harnessing the power of science, education, and stewardship.

Remember, wherever you go outdoors and for whatever reason, it is your responsibility to protect it. By minimizing our impact, we can safeguard our ability to enjoy the outdoors for years to come.

Principle 1: Plan Ahead and Prepare

Effective planning and preparation for a backcountry trip can help you achieve your objectives while minimizing environmental damage. Conversely, poor planning often leads to unpleasant experiences and harm to natural and cultural resources. Park rangers frequently encounter campers who have put themselves and the backcountry at risk due to inadequate planning and unexpected conditions.

Why is trip planning crucial? It ensures the safety of both individuals and groups, promotes Leave No Trace principles, reduces resource damage, and enhances the chances of achieving trip goals and learning about nature.

When planning a trip, consider these seven factors:

Defining your trip goals

Assessing participants' skills and abilities

Learning about the area from maps and literature

Choosing appropriate equipment and clothing

Matching activities with goals and abilities

Assessing the trip afterward

Identifying changes for next time

Other elements to consider include weather, terrain, regulations and restrictions, private land boundaries, group size, and anticipated food consumption and waste. Ensure the group size meets regulations, trip purpose, and Leave No Trace criteria.

Principle 2: Travel & Camp on Durable Surfaces

You will need to move through natural areas without causing harm to the environment. It's important to understand how travel can cause damage in order to achieve this goal. Travel damage occurs when plants and animals are trampled beyond repair, leading to soil erosion and the formation of unwanted trails.

Although trails have an impact on the land, they're necessary to prevent the development of multiple routes that can damage the environment. Sticking to one well-designed route rather than many poorly chosen paths is better. Hikers should use the trail as much as possible and avoid cutting switchbacks.

If hikers take breaks along the trail, they should provide space for other travelers. If they decide to move off-trail for breaks, they should follow the principles of off-trail travel.

Principle 3: Dispose of Waste Properly

It's important to get rid of human waste properly to prevent pollution, disease, and negative impacts on others. The best way to do this is to bury solid waste, but sometimes you must pack it out, like in narrow river canyons. Check with land management agencies for specific rules. Dig cat holes at least 200 feet away from water, trails, and camp in a spot where people are unlikely to go. Use a small garden trowel to dig a hole that is 6-8 inches deep. It needs to be at least 4-6 inches wide, then cover it up with natural materials. In the end, always make sure to pack out all your trash and inspect your campsite before leaving.

Principle 4: Leave What You Find

Don't take anything that belongs to a historic place or culture. You can examine and photograph but do not touch. Don't move or take things like rocks or plants that belong in nature.

Avoid introducing or transporting non-native species. Don't bring plants or animals to a place where they don't usually live. Don't make any new things like buildings or furniture or dig holes in the ground.

Principle 5: Minimize Campfire Impacts

Campfires were once necessary for cooking and warmth, but overuse has damaged many areas. Efficient camp stoves are now preferred for cooking and are essential for minimum-impact camping. Stoves are fast, flexible, and can be used in almost any weather condition.

Before deciding to build a fire, consider the potential damage to the backcountry. Check the fire danger for the time of year and location, look for administrative restrictions, and ensure there is enough wood without causing noticeable damage.

Principle 6: Respect Wildlife

It's important not to disturb animals or plants just to get a better look. It would be best if you observed wildlife from a distance, so they feel safe and aren't scared away. Even if some animals seem okay with you being close, keeping your distance is best because animals can be unpredictable. It will also help keep you and your pets safe.

Feeding animals with human food can harm their health, disrupt their habits, and create conflicts between humans and wildlife. You must store food, trash, and other scented items where animals can't reach them to avoid these problems. Animals should have easy access to water sources without feeling threatened by humans, so camps should be at least

200 feet away from water sources unless the land manager says otherwise.

Principle 7: Be Considerate of Others

In order to feel more in sync with nature, it's best to go in small groups, limit contact with others, and act respectfully. Avoid going on holidays or busy weekends or going during the off-season. That is when there are fewer people.

Technology can play a significant role in outdoor activities, but some people prefer to keep it minimal. Whatever your preference, it's important to be considerate of others. Many people come to listen to nature, so excessive noise, pets, and damage can detract from the natural beauty of the outdoors.

Conclusion

You may think this adventure was quite long, but I'm happy that we have reached the part of our book where I tell you how to act outdoors. This means that you have already set your mind to camping and hiking and plan to engage in it.

Still, it is crucial that you take part in the leave no trace principles since this is the basis of every outdoor activity. I hope you understand the importance of these rules so that you, as a hiker, preserve the environment. Together we can minimize all the negative impacts we have done so far on nature and Banff National Park. Finally, since we are at the end of our journey, we are now going to conclude what we have talked about so far.

CONCLUSION

I hope you see now that this guidebook didn't just give you hiking information. No, we explored the deeper benefits of spending time in nature and gave insights into how nature can reduce stress, improve mental health, and provide us with a sense of purpose and fulfillment. This information is not often found in other hiking guidebooks.

I hope I have helped you develop practical hiking skills, get confidence in your abilities, and feel empowered. Now you're ready to tackle new challenges! I have structured this book to cater to all levels of hikers and provided detailed trail information which you might need, as well as some practical tips for safe and efficient hiking. There are insights into hiking with your whole group too!

But that isn't all! The goal of this book and any book I write is to help people. I want you to escape the stresses of daily life and finally find adventure and achieve a sense of balance through nature.

Now let's go through our chapters: Our first chapter introduced Banff National Park and discussed all the benefits of hiking and spending time in nature. It was an introduction to our long journey together. After that, following the essential safety considerations, trail selection, and planning tips.

After that, we dealt with the essential logistics we needed to know before visiting this national park, like accommodation options, transportation, required passes, and the best time to visit. Finally came the big jump. We dove into beginner hikes, slowly drifted into intermediate hikes, and finally talked about the most challenging hikes in this National Park.

After talking about the recommended hikes in Banff National Park, I decided it might be dull hiking alone. That is why I gave you a guide to hiking with the whole pack while including children and dogs too. Still, our goal is not to leave anything behind, and that is why the last chapter discussed the importance of the leave-no-trace principles while camping and hiking.

And I can't even tell you how happy I am that we are here. I am sure you will love hiking. It is because hiking revived my zest for life. It became a source of peace and rejuvenation for me. It is a stairway to heaven amidst the stresses of modern living.

I love being surrounded by the stunning beauty of Banff, and I'm sure you will love this too. Now imagine yourself sitting upon a lookout, right above a milky, turquoise-colored lake, looking towards numerous mountain peaks barely covered with snow and lush forests below. That could be you enjoying your time in Banff.

It doesn't matter who you're hiking with, be it your friends or family, or even it could be you and your dog. Make sure you make the most of every moment! Savor the beauty of Banff National Park!

I hope this book will help you do so and push you to finally join the outdoor revolution.

LEAVE A REVIEW

In the end, if you have enjoyed my book, how I have written it, the information I gave you, and anything else for that matter, please don't hesitate to tell me. Please do so by contacting me or leaving a review of my book on Amazon!

RESOURCES

10Adventures. (n.d.). Fenland Trail Hike. Retrieved from https://www.10adventures.com/hikes/banff-national-park/fenland-trail

10Adventures. (n.d.). Johnston Canyon Hike. Retrieved from https://www.10adventures.com/hikes/banff/johnston-canyon

10Adventures. (n.d.). Johnston Canyon to Ink Pots Snowshoeing. Retrieved from https://www.10adventures.com/snowshoeing/banff-national-park/johnston-canyon-to-ink-pots

10Adventures. (n.d.). Lake Agnes Tea House Hike. Retrieved from https://www.10adventures.com/hikes/lake-louise/lake-agnes-tea-house

10Adventures. (n.d.). Lake Louise Lakeshore Hike. Retrieved from https://www.10adventures.com/hikes/banff-national-park/lake-louise-lakeshore

10Adventures. (n.d.). Moraine Lake Rockpile and Lakeshore Hike. Retrieved from https://www.10adventures.com/hikes/lake-louise/moraine-lake-rockpile-and-lakeshore

10Adventures. (n.d.). Plain of the Six Glaciers Hike. Retrieved from https://www.10adventures.com/hikes/lake-louise/plain-of-the-6-glaciers

10Adventures. (n.d.). Big Beehive Hike. Retrieved from https://www.10adventures.com/hikes/banff-national-park/big-beehive

10Adventures. (n.d.). Devil's Thumb Scramble. Retrieved from https://www.10adventures.com/scrambling/banff-national-park/devils-thumb

Adventures. (n.d.). Johnston Canyon Hike. Retrieved from https://www.10adventures.com/hikes/banff/johnston-canyon

Allswell Alert. (n.d.). 11 Essential Hiking Safety Tips You Should Always Follow.

Allswell Alert Blog. Retrieved from https://allswellalert.com/blog/11-essential-hiking-safety-tips-you-should-always-follow

American Hiking Society. (n.d.). 10 Essentials. Retrieved from https://americanhiking.org/resources/10essentials

American Hiking Society. (n.d.). Hiking Resources. Retrieved from https://americanhiking.org/hiking-resources

Banff & Lake Louise Tourism. (n.d.). Accommodation. Retrieved from https://www.banfflakelouise.com/accommodation

Banff & Lake Louise Tourism. (n.d.). Banff Hiking Essentials. Retrieved from https://www.travelbanffcanada.com/banff-hiking-essentials

Banff and Beyond. (n.d.). Options for Getting to the Canadian Rocky Mountains. Retrieved from http://banffandbeyond.com/options-getting-canadian-rocky-mountains

Banff and Beyond. (n.d.). Using Cell Phones and WiFi in the Canadian Rockies. Retrieved from http://banffandbeyond.com/using-cell-phones-and-wifi-in-the-canadian-rockies

Banff and Beyond. (n.d.). When Is the Best Time to Visit Banff National Park and the Rocky Mountains? Retrieved from http://banffandbeyond.com/when-is-the-best-time-to-visit-banff-national-park-and-the-rocky-mountains

Banff National Park. (n.d.). How to Get Here. Parks Canada. Retrieved from https://banffnationalpark.com/how-to-get-here

Banff National Park. (n.d.). In National Geographic Travel. Retrieved from https://www.nationalgeographic.com/travel/article/banff-canada-park

Banff National Park. (n.d.). In Britannica. Retrieved from https://www.britannica.com/place/Banff-National-Park

Family First K9. (n.d.). The Benefits of Hiking with Your Dog. Retrieved from https://familyfirstk9.com/the-benefits-of-hiking-with-your-dog

Fuller, K. (n.d.). 11 health benefits of hiking. Bearfoot Theory. Retrieved from https://bearfoottheory.com/benefits-of-hiking

Hiking Project. (n.d.). Overview of Hiking Project Features. Retrieved from https://www.hikingproject.com/help/21/overview-of-site-name-features

McManus, P. (2021, June 22). 9 Reasons Hiking Is Amazing for Kids. Carolina Country. Retrieved from https://www.carolinacountry.com/extras/digital-extras/9-reasons-hiking-is-amazing-for-kids

National Park Service. (n.d.). Benefits of hiking. U.S. Department of the Interior. Retrieved from https://www.nps.gov/subjects/trails/benefits-of-hiking.htm

National Park Service. (n.d.). Hiking with Kids. U.S. Department of the Interior. Retrieved from https://www.nps.gov/subjects/trails/hiking-with-kids.htm

Parks Canada. (n.d.). Backcountry. Retrieved from https://parks.canada.ca/pn-np/ab/banff/activ/arrierepays-backcountry

Parks Canada. (n.d.). Camping. Retrieved from https://parks.canada.ca/pn-np/ab/banff/activ/camping

Parks Canada. (n.d.). oTENTik. Retrieved from https://parks. canada.ca/pn-np/ab/banff/activ/camping/otentik

Parks Canada. (n.d.). Passes. Retrieved from https://parks.canada. ca/pn-np/ab/banff/visit/passer-passes

Parks Canada. (n.d.). Hiking: Know Before You Go [PDF]. Retrieved from https://www.fs.usda.gov/Internet/FSE_DOCUMENTS/ fseprd495156.pdf

REI Co-op. (n.d.). Hiking with Dogs: Expert Advice. Retrieved from https://www.rei.com/learn/expert-advice/hiking-dogs.html

REI Co-op. (n.d.). Hiking with Kids: Expert Advice. Retrieved from https://www.rei.com/learn/expert-advice/kids-hiking.html

The Banff Blog. (n.d.). Banff Park Pass – What You Need to Know. Retrieved from https://thebanffblog.com/banff-park-pass

The Wildest. (n.d.). Essential Hiking Gear for Dogs: A Comprehensive Guide. Retrieved from https://www.thewildest. com/dog-lifestyle/essential-hiking-gear-dogs

The Wildest. (n.d.). Tips for Hiking with Your Dog. Retrieved from https://www.thewildest.com/dog-lifestyle/ tips-hiking-with-your-dog

Tracks and Trails. (n.d.). Hiking for Kids on National Hiking Day. Retrieved from https://www.tracks-and-trails.com/blog/ hiking-for-kids-on-national-hiking-day

Travel Tomorrow. (2022, April 25). 10 Rules of Hiking. Retrieved from https://traveltomorrow.com/10-rules-of-hiking

Trekology. (n.d.). 5 Benefits of Hiking with Children. Retrieved from https://trekology.com/blogs/ hiking-and-trekking/5-benefits-of-hiking-with-children

U.S. Forest Service. (2017). Hiking: Know Before You Go [PDF]. Retrieved from https://www.fs.usda.gov/Internet/FSE_DOCUMENTS/fseprd495156.pdf

University of Minnesota. (n.d.). How does nature impact our wellbeing? Taking Charge of Your Health & Wellbeing. Retrieved from https://www.takingcharge.csh.umn.edu/how-does-nature-impact-our-wellbeing

Voices of Youth. (n.d.). Our disconnection from nature. Retrieved from https://www.voicesofyouth.org/blog/our-disconnection-nature

Wag! (n.d.). Dog Walking 101: Etiquette Rules for Hiking Trails. Retrieved from https://wagwalking.com/daily/dog-walking-101-etiquette-rules-for-hiking-trails

Ward, W. (2021, August 4). Hiking and Backpacking Safety Tips. Verywell Fit. Retrieved from https://www.verywellfit.com/hiking-and-backpacking-safety-tips-3119265

Wilson, A. (2021, August 17). Hiking with Kids: Tips and Essential Gear. TripSavvy. Retrieved from https://www.tripsavvy.com/hiking-with-kids-5179852

Wilson, A. (2021, August 30). Everything to Know About Hiking with Your Dog.

TripSavvy. Retrieved from https://www.tripsavvy.com/everything-to-know-about-hiking-with-your-dog-5180119

Wilson, A. (2022, January 7). Essential Safety Tips for Every Hike. TripSavvy. Retrieved from https://www.tripsavvy.com/essential-safety-tips-for-every-hike-5176614

File:Mirror Lake, looking up at Big Beehive (32324573171). jpg - Wikimedia Commons. (2016, August 30). https://commons.wikimedia.org/wiki/File:Mirror_Lake,_looking_

up_at_Big_Beehive._Yep,_I_climbed_that_son-of-a-bitch!_%2832324573171%29.jpg

Hacker, R. (2022, September 6). Lake Louise in Banff National Park · Free Stock Photo. Pexels. https://www.pexels.com/photo/lake-louise-in-banff-national-park-13527648/

Reimer, J. (2019, July 16). Beautiful View of Moraine Lake · Free Stock Photo. Pexels. https://www.pexels.com/photo/beautiful-view-of-moraine-lake-2662116/

Tarpey, W. (2020, September 7). snow covered mountain under blue sky during daytime. Unsplash.https://unsplash.com/photos/ZLrwRtv3Oos?utm_source=unsplash&utm_medium=referral&utm_content=creditShareLink

Reimer, J. (2020, September 29). Red Chairs on the Field · Free Stock Photo. Pexels. https://www.pexels.com/photo/red-chairs-on-the-field-2718054/

Wikimedia Commons. (2022, December). https://commons.wikimedia.org/wiki/File:Banffmapv2.jpg

Made in the USA
Middletown, DE
10 April 2024

52816956R00086